# SPIRIT OF THE *IROQUOIS*

# Spirit of the *Iroquois*

Len Taphouse

The Pentland Press
Edinburgh – Cambridge – Durham – USA

First published in 1995 by
The Pentland Press Ltd
1 Hutton Close,
South Church
Bishop Auckland
Durham



ISBN 1-85821-314-2

Typeset by Carnegie Publishing, 18 Maynard St, Preston
Printed and bound in Great Britain by Bookcraft (Bath) Ltd.

*To all the men who sailed in the* Iroquois

# CONTENTS

# PREFACE

THIS story starts with a dedication to the marine engineers and those that sailed on the *Iroquois*, and progresses with the early ideas of the origins of the tanker as we now know it. This is followed by the complete history of the two ships. This is a factual account and in most cases has been checked through more than one source. To complete the history there is a complete set of the voyage record cards so that the reader can trace all the movements of the *Iroquois*.

This is followed by the family tree and my father's upbringing. I have made an attempt to show that although the family had a poor background, his mother's wisdom prevailed, and the whole family made successful livings.

The story progresses through his career at sea and on to the ship he regarded as HIS, the *Iroquois*. This was in many ways a unique ship, and I have traced out its history from conception to scrapping. I still believe she was blessed with good fortune. Very few tankers survived two world wars.

My father had a love of ships' engines and would never miss an opportunity, when on board a ship, to visit the engine room. When he retired from work, he said his happiness would have been complete if only he had one of the engines from the *Iroquois* in the back garden. His interest in engines and copper-work never died. He built me a model single-cylinder, single-acting steam engine when I was about fifteen. It wasn't till I was in the second year of my apprenticeship that I was able to connect it to the air-line at work and see it run. It was another thirty years later that I built my first steam engine.

The section entitled 'Stories of His Ships' relates only to stories he told us (usually over the meal table) about life at sea. Some of these I have been able to verify, and those that have been verified invariably carry a date.

The copper plate and matchbox still exist today.

From the various letters that I have received from different people who knew the *Iroquois* in the 1920s and 30s, the memory of her still lives on.

# SHIPS MENTIONED IN THIS STORY

SS *Chesapeake* (1) 1895, Glasgow, 4,521 tons, Glasgow, Anglo-Am.
MV *Chesapeake* (2) 1928, Belfast, 8,955 tons, Belfast, Anglo-Am.
Named after Chesapeake Bay, NE coast of U.S.A.
SS *Cheyenne* (1) 1908, Newcastle, 4,987 tons, Newcastle, Anglo-Am.
MV *Cheyenne* (2) 1930, Newcastle, 8,825 tons, Newcastle, Anglo-Am.
Named after a Red Indian tribe.
SS *Delaware* 1893, Glasgow, 2,469 tons, London, Anglo-Am.
Named after Delaware Bay, NE coast of U.S.A.
SS *Genesee* 1889, Newcastle, 1,839 tons, London, Anglo-Am.
Named after a Red Indian tribe
SS *Gluckauf* 1886, Newcastle, 2,307 tons, Geestemunde, Deutsche Americk Petroleum. Translated from the German: 'Good Luck'.
SS *Iroquois* 1908, Belfast, 5,772 tons, Belfast, Anglo-Am.
Named after a Red Indian tribe.
SS *Laconia*, armed merchant cruiser, Newcastle, 19,695 tons, Cunard White Star.
SS *Navahoe* 1907, Belfast, 6,969 tons, Belfast, Anglo-Am.
Named after a Red Indian tribe.
SS *Narragansett* (1) 1903, Greenock, 9,196 tons, Greenock, Anglo-Am.
MV *Narragansett* (2) 1920, Barrow, 6,889 tons, Barrow, Anglo-Am.
Named after an inlet on the SE coast of Rhode Island.
SS *Saranac* 1918, Newcastle, 7,555 tons, Newcastle, Anglo-Am.
SS *Suwanee* 1888, Newcastle, 2,075 tons, London, Anglo-Am.
Named after a Red Indian tribe.
SS *Tamarac* (1) 1908, Sunderland, 3,318 tons, Glasgow, Anglo-Am.
SS *Tamarac* (2) 1916, Newcastle, 5,042 tons, Newcastle, Anglo-Am.
Named after a suburb of Ford Lauderdale.
SS *Tuscarora* 1917, Sunderland, 4,473 tons, Sunderland, Anglo-Am.
Named after an American river.
SS *Voltaire* 1923, armed merchant cruiser, Belfast, 13,301 tons, Belfast, Lamport and Holt.
SS *Wapello* 1912, Sunderland, 3,369 tons, Newcastle, Anglo-Am.
Named after a town in Idaho.

# THOSE THAT GO DOWN TO THE SEA IN SHIPS

THESE stories are really meant as a tribute to my father and those seldom mentioned, the Marine Engineers. In time of war, deck officers are mentioned in dispatches, as often being the dare-doing, courageous, and pushy types. The engineers down below, often working in terrible conditions of heat and grime, are even more rarely decorated. Yet in times of war, they are invariably the last to leave the ship, as the engine-rooms are sealed off in times of conflict. The Chief Engineer is the one that the deck officers turn to when they are in an emergency situation, and it is sometimes his decision that sends a ship into dry dock, or stops the ship because of a mishap. It is the engineers who work unceasingly (sometimes to the point of collapse) to effect a repair.

In reading maritime books and, in particular, war at sea books, I have comes across a few quotes that I feel are worthy of mention:

'. . . and the chief engineer led an engine-room team that coped with fire and flood, water in the fuel tanks, salt in the feed water lines, and all the gremlins that haunted an overworked ship that was due for a refit.'

'The engineers went to work trying to forget the hollow crashes of bombs falling close by and the stark fact that at any moment the sea might invade the dimly lit trap of the engine-room.'

'The second and third engineers crawled through bilges to the valves which would connect up the steam fuel pumps to replace the broken electric pumps. Meanwhile the junior engineer wriggled his way over the boiler casing looking for fractures.'

From 1900 onwards there were a few unscrupulous shipowners about; my father told me that the Greek owners were amongst the worst. They often sent ships to sea that were completely unseaworthy, knowing that they would founder, just to collect the insurance money. I said to him that surely there were no British shipowners that were like that. His reply was that there were three British companies (known as the three bad Rs) that used to operate the same way. They did however buy some new ships. They were ordered from a well-known Tyne shipbuilders, that used to build cut-price ships and undercut all the other shipbuilders. Instead of using one-inch-thick plate they used ¾-inch plate instead, and most of their ships were underpowered. This caused them to fare badly when they encountered bad weather. Anglo-American Oil Co did not come into this class. From what my father said, and uncles told me, they were reasonable employers and certainly looked after their ships. Very few Anglo-American Oil Co ships foundered other than in time of war. Although several of their steamers lasted for about forty years, they were kept in good shape and continued to give good service.

# LIFE AT SEA

WORKING conditions for crew members in the years leading up to the 1920s were poor. They were engaged literally only a few hours before the ship sailed and (with some companies) they had to supply their own food for the voyage or buy it from the ship's cook. Very few ships in those days carried refrigerators, and in consequence many stomach disorders occurred as a result of eating rotten meat and food that had gone off. The crew members had to supply their own mattress and blankets. The mattress was usually filled with straw that they had bought from the ship's chandler as they joined the ship. The straw mattresses were more commonly known as 'donkey breakfasts'. By the end of each trip this straw had invariably disintegrated to chaff and was somewhat soiled and therefore had to be replaced. Cooking was carried out on a coal-fired stove situated in the middle of the crew's quarters, where the space was shared by about six men. Very little overtime was ever paid to members of the crew, but they were often called on to work extended hours.

Crew members were paid off within hours of reaching a home port—not always the port where they had signed on, necessitating yet more expense in reaching home. On several occasions records show that sailors had fallen ill while still in the Thames Estuary and were put ashore by tug or by the pilot vessel off Dover, rather than be treated like sick passengers. Quite often crew members had their pay stopped when they were taken ill at sea. Records also show that generally speaking captains and first mates were quite concerned about the health and well-being of crew members. On occasions captains had been known to set broken legs and limbs and stitch up wounds. When in port, where possible a doctor would be called or a crewman would be put into hospital. Generally speaking as much as could be done, was done.

The poor conditions prevailing at sea had an adverse effect of the morale of crewmen. Arguments between crew were common and on occasions fights broke out. Extreme violence such as stabbing resulted in the guilty party being locked away in a storeroom, that was unlit, and fed on (literally) bread and water. On arrival in port the offender was handed over to the British Consul.

The case-oil trade existed up to about 1915. It consisted of oil that was carried in barrels and in consequence gave a two-way trade, the return voyage being made with empty barrels. Later came the true case oil, which was oil (usually used for lighting and heating) which was packed, eight at a time, in cases. The case oil carriers were generally similar to conventional cargo ships, the cargo being winched out of the holds and into barges or quays. In very remote ports they were lowered into small boats and rowed ashore where the cases were then manhandled.

The life of a ship's officer, whether Engineer or Deck, tended to be very different. Both branches had gone through a period of training, invariably five years. In this apprenticeship they had had to respond to the discipline associated with training, and arguments between officers were rare. The phrase 'officer and gentleman' had some credence. While they may not all have been gentlemen, they were invariably good managers of men. The conditions that they worked under were vastly superior to those of the crew. All officers signed contracts (articles) with the shipping company which did in fact give them a security. In those days the articles were for three years. Between 1909 and 1915 Anglo-American Oil Co was busy building up a fleet of ships in the Far East, known as Tank Storage and Carriage Co, and many of the officers of Anglo ships found themselves on ships that travelled to the Far East and then were transferred to Tank Storage, with the result that they actually stayed away from the UK for three years. The ship itself stayed in the Far East and was then crewed by Chinamen.

Junior engineer officers and junior deck officers often shared cabins, usually two to a cabin. Third engineers and second mates and upwards invariably had their own cabins. Meals for officers were provided by the company at the company's expense. On some occasions on some ships even overtime was paid for officers who did more than the standard fifty-six hours a week; however in these cases written evidence of its necessity was always made by the superior officer. Officers were given two weeks' leave a year. With Anglo-American they tended to be a bit more generous, and allowed each officer one round trip off each year.

All cabins occupied by officers were furnished with a bunk and settee as well as a desk and wardrobe. They were also provided with large hooks on opposite bulkheads; this was for the slinging of hammocks. These tended to be a popular sleeping arrangement in the Far East. All officers had a steward to look after them. The Captain and the Chief Engineer each had a personal steward. The duty of the stewards was to keep the cabins clean, change the bedding and serve meals to the officers in the saloon. In most cases the steward would bring cups of tea to watch-keepers during their watch-keeping periods.

When a ship dry-docked for repairs, the officers stayed with the ship, but were often able to manage to slip home for the weekend. There tended to be more contentment amongst officers, and fighting was unknown.

'All hands on deck' is a well-known saying. On board all ships is a klaxon horn which is a signal from the engine-room that help is urgently required. When this was sounded anyone who was asleep off-watch would instantly be woken up by the din, and would rush down to the engine-room. If the breakdown was serious they would stay down there till the repairs were complete.

With the advent of the First World War, conditions for all those at sea changed. Shipping Acts for deep sea vessels altered to the extent that all those at sea in what was considered a war zone were paid extra money. Food for crewmen was paid for by the company and they generally had a standard working week, hence there were overtime payments. By this time America was considered to be the country flowing with milk and honey and many crewmen jumped ship to begin a new life in the USA. In the following years there were other major changes in the design of ships. There was the changeover from coal-firing to oil-burning. This meant a drastic reduction in the numbers of firemen. In many ships the complement of firemen dropped from twenty-four to six.

In some ships (not Anglo-Am) the owners were so tight-fisted that when in port, boilers were shut down when the steam winches were stopped for the day, and therefore the generators came to a standstill and the ship was plunged into darkness. Candles paid for by the crew became the only method of lighting. Many ships that were built up to the 1920s were still not equipped with electricity. This was a throwback to the days of sail, when oil lanterns were the norm. However, these ships carried a lamp-trimmer whose job it was to ensure that the lamps were in good working order and lit at the appropriate time. Because of the potential fire hazard, oil lamps were quickly dispensed with and electric lighting became the norm on tankers. Life on tankers always carried the potential hazard of fire, and a fire on a tanker is probably the most disastrous thing at sea. Generally oil tanker operators paid better wages than general cargo operators and passenger liner companies. The social aspects of working on tankers were poorer. Cargo steamers discharged only during the hours of daylight and by virtue of the cargo they carried would invariably be in port either discharging or loading sometimes for a couple of weeks. Tankers on the other hand discharged continuously till empty, and often tank cleaning was carried out on the vessel when she was at sea. By the 1920s pumping arrangements had improved so much. Not only were the ship's pumps used in discharging, but shore-based pumps as well. Thus all tankers were in on one tide and out on the next, giving little time for officers to slip off home.

In the early 1930s many ships were laid up; almost a quarter of the world's tankers were amongst the lay-ups. Some of the favourite lay-up spots have come into use again in the 1990s. They are the River Fal in Cornwall and the River Blackwater in Essex. Generally speaking, when a ship was laid up the Captain, Chief Engineer and two crewmen were kept on board; this compliance reduced the insurance rates. The lay-ups caused further redundancies.

With the coming of World War II and the need for all ships to be pressed into service, many men were only too pleased to get back to sea. Conditions by then had improved so much that very few men jumped ship during World War II. Many people do not realize that German raiders were built with the sole intention of destroying Allied shipping, and a U-boat considered the sinking of a 10,000-ton loaded tanker more prestigious than the sinking of a destroyer.

The U-boats hunted in packs just to track down convoys. Destroyers, frigates and other men-o-war were just hindrances that they had to put up with, and invariably U-boats would run away from them. After the war there was a massive rebuilding programme. Each shipping company tried to replace its war losses and many of the older vessels like the *Iroquois* were sent to the scrap-yard. Some of them had mounted up forty years' service. The technique of shipbuilding changed after the war. It was learnt from the building of the Liberty ship, that a ship could be successfully all-welded. This technique produced a lighter ship. Ships built after the war were powered by either steam turbine or diesel engines. It was realized that the reciprocating steam engine (usually a triple expansion) was heavy and inefficient, its fuel consumption was twice that of the steam turbine, and the turbine always had a higher power output. Diesel engines for main power of the 1950s were still proving rather unreliable, and their maintenance costs were very high although their running costs were low. In the 1950s it was common for a grain ship to be discharged by grain elevators that would discharge 5,000 tons of grain in four hours. The engineers and pumpmen would work continuous watches in port to keep the ship trimmed.

Again the design of ships changed dramatically. The supertanker was born. In 1960 a supertanker was about 30,000 tons, often single-engined with a total ship's company of about thirty. A few years later tankers of 100,000 tons were being built. The early ones of the 1970s still being driven by steam turbines, the changes in diesel engine design with the use of nickel-chrome steels drastically reduced the number of breakdowns of the motor (diesel) ships and spelt the death of the steamships. A further move was the use of boiler oil in motor ships. In the 1960s all manoeuvring was done on the engines using diesel oil, but after full-way they changed over to boiler oil as this was considerably cheaper. By the 1980s engines were designed to run specifically on boiler oil; this had however to be heated before it could be used. Former engines that were known as diesel were now known as heavy oil engines. Nowadays engine breakdowns are a thing of the past.

All these changes unfortunately had an effect on Engineer Officers. Up to the 1970s all Engineer Officers were drawn from the engineering industry. A would-be engineer had to have served a minimum training of four years or had to go through a cadet engineering scheme. He would generally start life at sea as an assistant engineer and would immediately stand watch as an assistant to the senior watch-keeper; the watches were as follows.

| | |
|---|---|
| 12–4 | Senior 3rd, and Junior 4th |
| 4–8 | 2nd Eng., and 5th Eng. |
| 8–12 | Junior 3rd, and Senior 4th. |

The Chief Engineer never stood watches except in the case of sickness, but was on call at all times. When a ship docked and the main engines were shut down all engineers came off watch and settled down to day work, with the exception of one of the two Junior Engineers, who worked nights from 2300 to 0700. The time in port for engineers was spent carrying out routine repairs. With the advent of larger ships and the bulk carriers and VLCC (Very Large Crude Carriers), life for the engineer changed yet again. Unmanned engine-rooms became the norm. With each pump came a back-up pump. In the event of a pump 'conking out' its back-up would automatically start up and a warning alarm would alert the engineers. All engineers were on day-work but were permanently on call. Generally shipping companies only allowed their employees to be away from home for about six months. All personnel were flown out to join a ship in a foreign port, and were repatriated in the same way.

With the demise of the shipbuilding yards of the UK more and more ships since 1980 have been built in the Far East. With more and more ships flying flags of convenience, more ships now took on crews from third world countries, thus reducing running costs still further. Containerisation still further reduced loading times. Container berths are purpose-built, and in 1992 Singapore port boasted that it could unload a 50,000-ton container ship in less than eight hours. VLCC also discharge oil through a discharge pipe that is nearly a metre in diameter.

# THE STORY OF THE TANKER

THE story of the tanker goes back to the late 1800s when oil was conveyed in barrels, in what were known as 'case oil ships'. This was a wasteful as well as a dangerous method of transportation. Wasteful because of the large amount of space between each of the barrels (honeycomb effect), as well as the amount of time in loading and unloading. It was dangerous because if any of the barrels became loose in transit, this could lead to a fire. It also meant either a return voyage with empty barrels, or the barrels had to be replaced for each cargo. The next development was to build a tanker with cylindrical tanks along its length that were welded onto a frame still with the honeycomb idea. These were pumped from one end for loading and discharging. At least this idea was much safer than the previous one, and certainly speeded up discharge.

The next idea was the original forerunner of the bulk oil carrier. Most of the barrelled oil was carried on sailing ships known as schooners, and oil companies were loath to move away from sailing ships; steam ships were new-fangled things. The 2,307-ton *Gluckauf* (translated means 'good luck') built in 1886, by Armstrong Mitchell, of Newcastle, and registered at Geestemunde for Deutsch-Amerik Petroleum, a Standard Oil Company German-affiliated company, was really the prototype of the modern tanker; she had two cargo holds which were built as tanks, and pumps in the engine room were used for loading and discharging cargo. She was equipped with sails that were of sufficient size to push her along at about three to four knots. To increase her speed or to allow her to continue (on becalmed days) she also had a coal-fired boiler and an engine connected to a screw that enabled her to move at a modest speed of about six knots.

In the United States of America there were a number of experiments being conducted by the Standard Oil Co where oil was transported by tanker barges. These were towed by tugs and these experiments were first conducted around the US coast, and very large volumes of tanker barges were moved in this way. The size of the barges was increased, and the idea still met with success. To progress the idea further, attempts were even made to tow barges across the Pacific Ocean. This proved successful but to attempt a North Atlantic crossing on a regular basis was an entirely different proposition.

*SS* Gluckauf.

Most shipowners were reluctant to see the approaching end of the sailing ships and hit on a compromise. Further steps were taken by adding sails to these barges, as the use of sails aided the towing operation, but each of the barges then had to be manned. This towing practice was a paying proposition and it was decided to try it on a larger scale for trans-ocean transportation. Standard Oil Co towed barges carrying a million-gallon cargo of naphtha and oil from New York to San Francisco via the Magellan Straits, Cape Horn, South America. This in turn led to the concept of the *Iroquois* and the *Navahoe* (named after Red Indian tribes), also known as the Horse and Cart of the Atlantic, or affectionately, as the 'Twins'.

In the early 1900s, the Anglo-American Oil Company, a British company registered in London in 1888 as a subsidiary of Standard Oil Co, were building up their fleet of oil tankers, and were pioneers in developing the early tankers. They soon had one of the largest sailing fleets in the world. It was the first company to run a regular oil fleet which was founded on twelve vessels, ships and barges of iron and steel. The largest of these at that time was the SS *Narrangansett* of 9,196 tons; built in 1903, she was 523 feet long. At the time she was the largest vessel ever to be built on the lower reaches of the Clyde.

The company found that they were responsible for the importing and distribution as well as the sale of three-quarters of all the oil and petrol that was used in Britain. Much of this oil was used as fuel oil in the generation of steam, which at that time was the main source of power. The Royal Navy also began to change over many of its ships to oil-fired boilers, and had ten oil-fired battleships before and during World War I. Apart from a few small destroyers and possibly one or two battlecruisers, all their ships were still coal-fired. The main changeover to oil-firing did not properly take place until post-war construction started.

Quote from the fuel figures of an 8,000 ton ship which was converted from a coal burner to an oil burner. Her fuel oil consumption was only 28–30 tons per day compared to coal consumption of 42–43 tons per day, but with six men doing the work of twenty-six needed in the stokehold with coal.

As the growth of business made it necessary to use outside charters at a time of high freight rates, in 1907 the partnership of the *Iroquois* and the *Navahoe* began. The *Navahoe* was the last vessel with sails that was built for Anglo-American Oil Co.

# THE *IROQUOIS*

THE *Narragansett* was at that time the largest tanker at 9,196 tons and was built in 1903 at Greenock, Scotland.

The *Iroquois* at 9,202 tons was slightly shorter than her consort the *Narragansett*, but was more beamy. She was launched on 27 June 1907 by Mrs Powell, wife of one of the directors of Harland and Wolff, Belfast. She was the first large tank steamer to be fitted with twin screws and was the only one ever designed and built principally to tow a barge of almost equal size. The *Iroquois* was 476′ 3″ in length, 60′ 3″ breadth and had a moulded depth of 35′ 5″.

At that time most ships were equipped with either compound expansion or triple expansion engines. The *Iroquois* was the first tanker to be equipped with two sets of quadruple expansion engines. With crankshaft journals of 12 inches and crank-pins of 12.75, the engines had bores of 21″, 30″, 48.5″, 62″ × 42″ stroke, this gave her a nominal horsepower of 748, a shaft horsepower of 1,500 and an indicated horsepower of 5,000, driving two 16ft-diameter propellers through a short stern tube of only 57″ length, on shafts 13 inches in diameter that had a pitch of fifteen feet.

These engines took steam from four single-ended oil-fired boilers that were sixteen feet in diameter and eleven feet long and had four furnaces each, and operated at 215 pounds per square inch, which in those days was considered high pressure. Although the original intention was that the *Iroquois* was to be built as a coal-burner, at some stage in her construction the decision to install oil-firing equipment was made. Most tanker owners waited till at least 1910 before moving to fuel oil. Shipowners in general left it till after the First World War. Anglo-American Oil Co ships traded between oil ports and therefore had no problems in bunkering. Only 3% of the world merchant tonnage was oil-burning in 1914, and of this, half was under the US flag. This had the effect of providing more accommodation space (where the bunkers would have been). These boilers consumed about sixty tons of oil per day. This gave her a speed of about twelve knots laden, and even when she was towing the *Navahoe* she maintained a speed in excess of ten and a half knots.

The engine-room was unique in other ways. All the handrails and stanchions were made from brass, and all the lubricating oil drip trays were made from either copper or brass.

The *Iroquois* was, in fact, the first large-tank steamer to have her propelling machinery situated aft. She had a cargo capacity of 8,888 tons and a bunker capacity of 2,000 tons. The oil cargo was contained in eighteen compartments, and an exceptionally complete oil pumping system powered by a 12-foot-diameter donkey boiler for loading and discharging was provided, as well as all the necessary appliances. This system was powerful enough to pump the oil cargo through three miles of piping.

It is interesting to note that Lloyds Register of Shipping states that she was even fitted with electric lights, although the *Gluckauf* was as well. How we take things for granted, but at that time electricity was still considered dangerous on a ship. Sparks caused by badly designed switchgear and equipment were thought to lead to fires. Most ships at that time were lit by oil lanterns, and this was considered to be even more dangerous on tankers.

She was very strongly built, with web frames, and one very notable feature of her strength was the double sheerstrake. The doubling plates were held together with a mass of rivets. The cellular double-bottom tanks were situated under the engine-room space and were used for the storage of fresh and boiler-feed water. She had a counter-stern which was typical of the design of the day. Her bows had very little shear and were not flared at all. She had a solid centre-line bulkhead from stem to stern even through the engine-room, and she was primarily built to tow the *Navahoe* (a barge of almost equal size). To do this she was equipped with special patent towing gear that was housed in a deckhouse on the poop deck.

Her fore-peak tank could hold 194 tons and her after-peak tank 340 tons. These tanks were designed to hold fresh water but were often used as cargo tanks.

She carried a foremast of 82' and a mainmast of 85', which were very tall for her tonnage. The masts had a 'traveller rail' fitted to the aft-facing side. It can only be assumed that they may have been used for some sort of auxiliary sail, although there is no proof of this.

Many of the ships of the *Iroquois* era had what was commonly known as a 'Woodbine stack' funnel. These were very high, thin funnels, as most of the boilers at that time were based on natural draught and required height to maintain the draught. The *Iroquois* boilers were operated by means of forced draught; in other words, the air consumed by the boilers was moved by means of fans driven by small steam engines. Because of this the *Iroquois* had a shorter stack than most vessels of her time.

The *Iroquois* was fitted with wireless several years after she was built, and it is believed that the *Iroquois* was the first tanker to be fitted with wireless. This may sound strange, but at that time only 139 merchant ships were fitted with wireless, and most of them were passenger ships. As designed, there was no specific 'radio room', therefore the pilot's cabin had to be used. It was immediately abaft the Master's bedroom and originally had access to the Master's bathroom. If the photos of the *Iroquois* of 1913 are compared with those of later dates it is evident that another bridge level was added. It is good guesswork to assume that this was done as an aid to viewing the *Navahoe*. This work was carried out at Rotterdam in 1920.

The *Iroquois* was provided with one of the most powerful searchlights in the world, with the object of being able to pick out the *Navahoe* during darkness. This searchlight was powered by a small Curtis turbine connected to a dynamo that was able to take a load of 200 amps at 125 volts. This appliance was situated in a recess at the after end of the starboard engine-room at main deck level. Anglo-American reckoned that the *Navahoe* would either drift or be driven away from the *Iroquois* in bad weather.

One of the other notable features of the *Iroquois* was its bridge, which had very large port-holes at its after end. This was to enable the bridge's officers to keep an eye on the tow at all times.

The ship's officers numbered twenty-seven, and the total ship's company varied between fifty and sixty. She had certified accommodation for 120 persons. The engine-room personnel were accommodated aft either side above the engine-room, and the deck officers and radio officers were accommodated amidships. The rest of the ship's crew were accommodated aft. She carried four 28' lifeboats as well as a small 20' motor cutter.

She left the fitting-out berth at Belfast on 21 October 1907 for sea trials, and dry-docked at Barry Island where her bottom was cleaned and coated. She left there on the 27th and commenced her maiden voyage on 28 October. She made an exceedingly good passage to New York, arriving there on 8 November. Her first cargo-carrying voyage was to Purfleet, where she arrived on 28 November. She was to make two more solo transatlantic trips before picking up the *Navahoe*.

Extract from the log 31/12/1907.

I hereby certify that at 4.35 am on 31/12/07 it was reported to the 1st Mate by one of the A.B.'s that one of the A.B.'s was missing, he not having returned to the forecastle after having been relieved at the wheel. A thorough search throughout the ship was made, but he could not be found. His cap was found (at daylight) on top of No. 8 tank lid. At about 4.05 am she had shipped a very heavy sea over the after deck and it is presumed it must have taken the A.B. overboard. He was only missed because he did not return to his bunk.

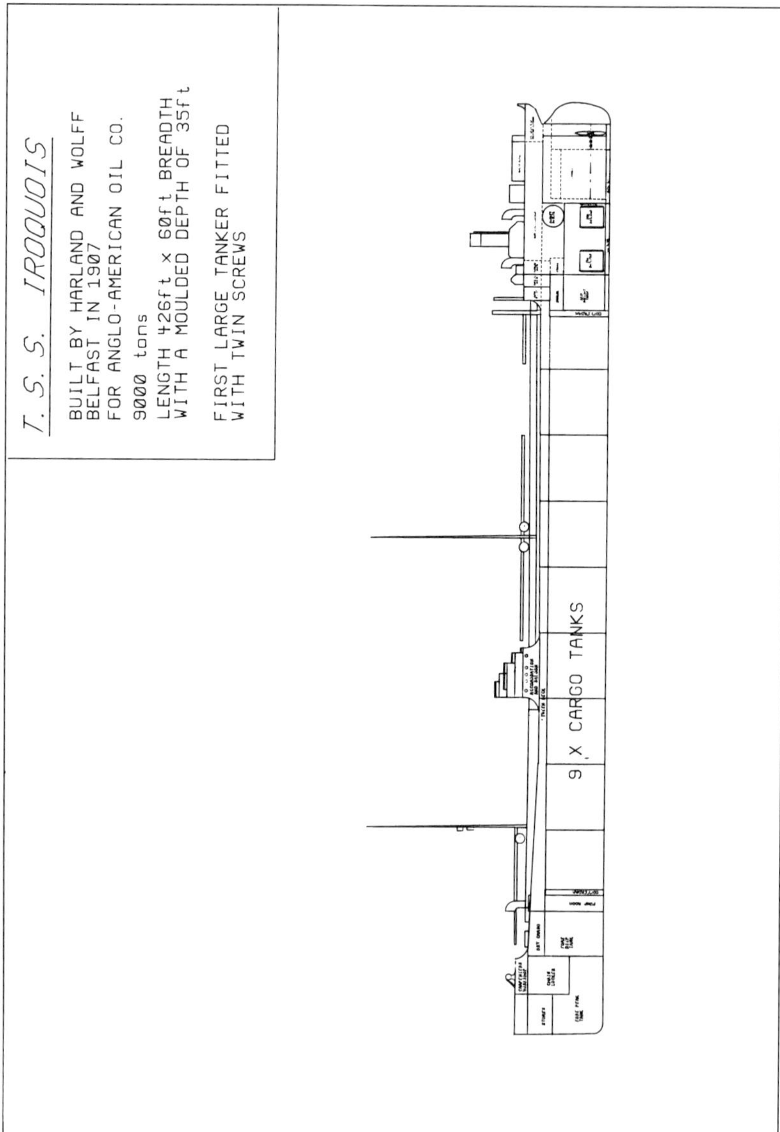
T. S. S. IROQUOIS
BUILT BY HARLAND AND WOLFF
BELFAST IN 1907
FOR ANGLO-AMERICAN OIL CO.
9000 tons
LENGTH 426ft x 60ft BREADTH
WITH A MOULDED DEPTH OF 35ft
FIRST LARGE TANKER FITTED
WITH TWIN SCREWS
9 X CARGO TANKS

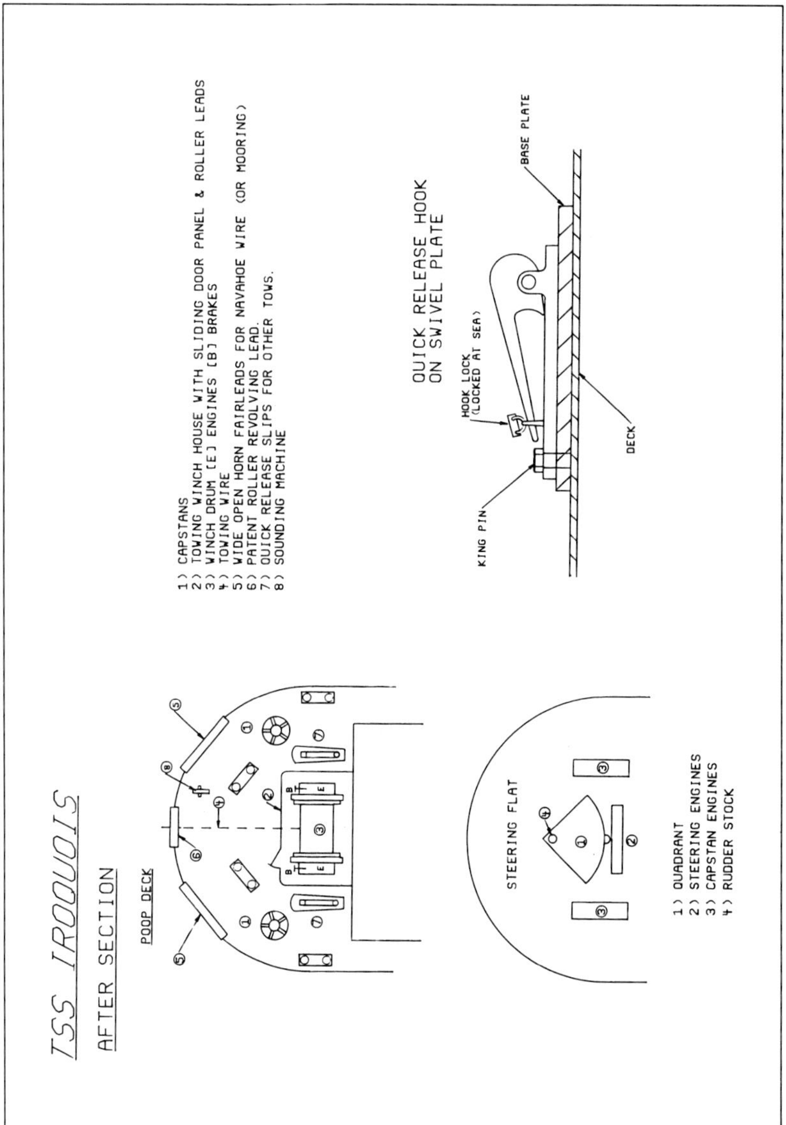
TSS IROQUOIS
AFTER SECTION
POOP DECK
1) CAPSTANS
2) TOWING WINCH HOUSE WITH SLIDING DOOR PANEL & ROLLER LEADS
3) WINCH DRUM [E] ENGINES [B] BRAKES
4) TOWING WIRE
5) WIDE OPEN HORN FAIRLEADS FOR NAVAHOE WIRE (OR MOORING)
6) PATENT ROLLER REVOLVING LEAD.
7) QUICK RELEASE SLIPS FOR OTHER TOWS.
8) SOUNDING MACHINE
QUICK RELEASE HOOK ON SWIVEL PLATE
BASE PLATE
HOOK LOCK (LOCKED AT SEA)
KING PIN
DECK
STEERING FLAT
1) QUADRANT
2) STEERING ENGINES
3) CAPSTAN ENGINES
4) RUDDER STOCK

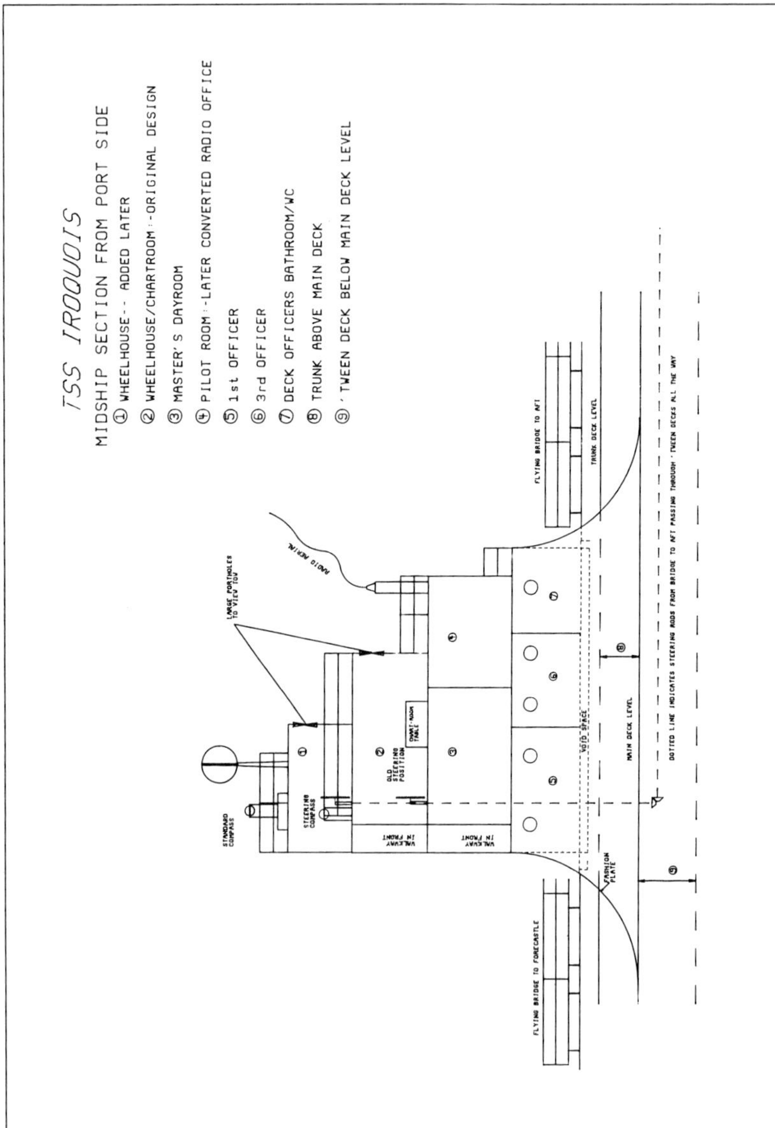
TSS IROQUOIS
MIDSHIP SECTION FROM PORT SIDE
① WHEELHOUSE - - ADDED LATER
② WHEELHOUSE/CHARTROOM : -ORIGINAL DESIGN
③ MASTER'S DAYROOM
④ PILOT ROOM : -LATER CONVERTED RADIO OFFICE
⑤ 1st OFFICER
⑥ 3rd OFFICER
⑦ DECK OFFICERS BATHROOM/WC
⑧ TRUNK ABOVE MAIN DECK
⑨ 'TWEEN DECK BELOW MAIN DECK LEVEL
STANDARD COMPASS
STEERING COMPASS
LARGE PORTHOLES TO VIEW TOW
RADIO AERIAL
OLD STEERING POSITION
CHART-ROOM TABLE
WALKWAY IN FRONT
WALKWAY IN FRONT
FLYING BRIDGE TO AFT
TRUNK DECK LEVEL
VOID SPACE
MAIN DECK LEVEL
FASHION PLATE
FLYING BRIDGE TO FORECASTLE
DOTTED LINE INDICATES STEERING RODS FROM BRIDGE TO AFT PASSING THROUGH 'TWEEN DECKS ALL THE WAY

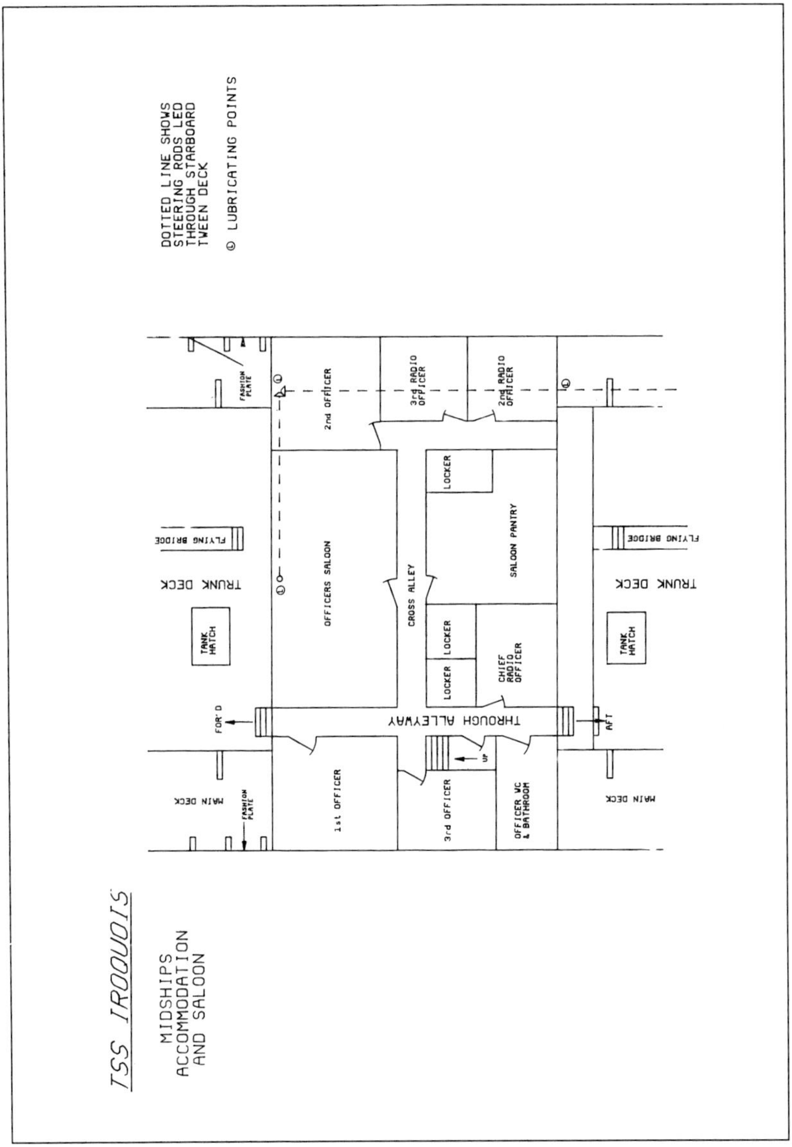
TSS IROQUOIS
MIDSHIPS
ACCOMMODATION
AND SALOON
DOTTED LINE SHOWS
STEERING RODS LED
THROUGH STARBOARD
TWEEN DECK
Ⓛ LUBRICATING POINTS
2nd OFFICER
3rd RADIO OFFICER
2nd RADIO OFFICER
FASHION PLATE
LOCKER
FLYING BRIDGE
OFFICERS SALOON
CROSS ALLEY
SALOON PANTRY
TRUNK DECK
TANK HATCH
LOCKER
LOCKER
LOCKER
CHIEF RADIO OFFICER
FOR'D
THROUGH ALLEYWAY
AFT
UP
MAIN DECK
FASHION PLATE
1st OFFICER
3rd OFFICER
OFFICER WC & BATHROOM

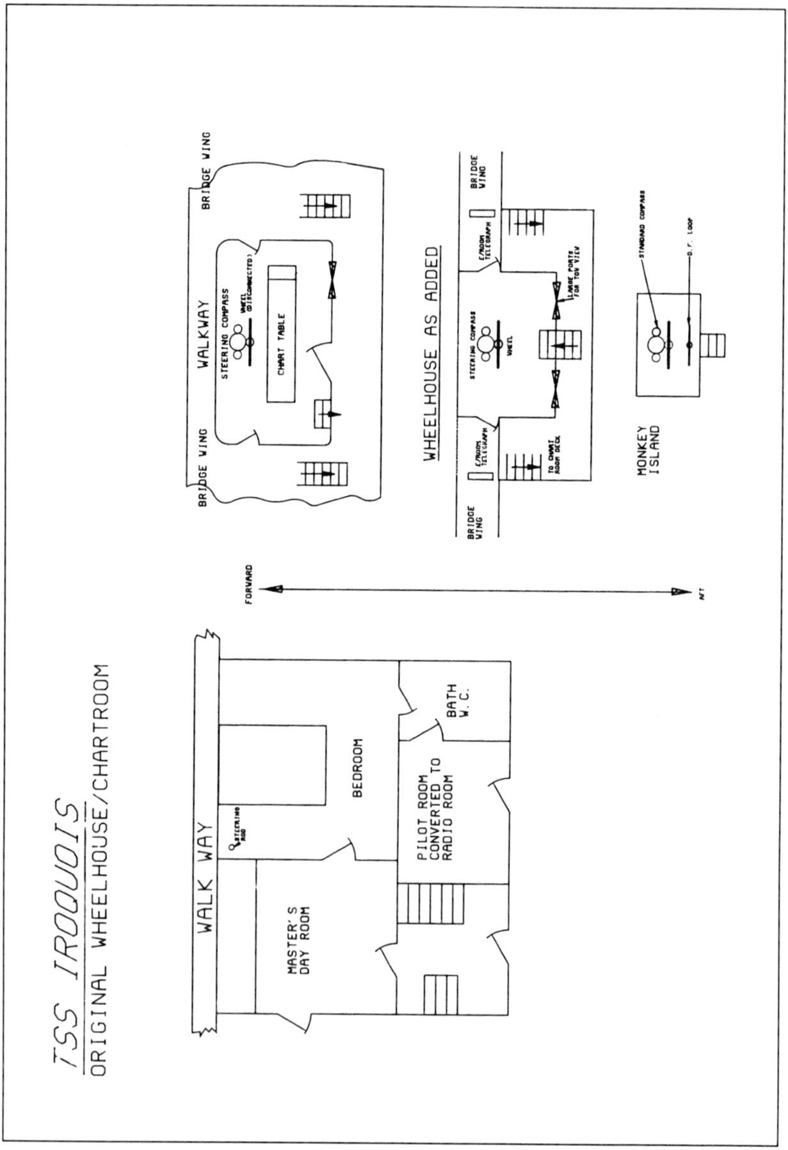
TSS IROQUOIS
ORIGINAL WHEELHOUSE/CHARTROOM
WALK WAY
MASTER'S DAY ROOM
BEDROOM
STEERING ROD
PILOT ROOM CONVERTED TO RADIO ROOM
BATH W.C.
FORWARD
AFT
BRIDGE WING
WALKWAY
STEERING COMPASS
WHEEL (DISCONNECTED)
CHART TABLE
BRIDGE WING
WHEELHOUSE AS ADDED
BRIDGE WING
E/ROOM TELEGRAPH
STEERING COMPASS
WHEEL
LARGE PORTS FOR TOW VIEW
E/ROOM TELEGRAPH
TO CHART ROOM DECK
BRIDGE WING
MONKEY ISLAND
STANDARD COMPASS
D.F. LOOP

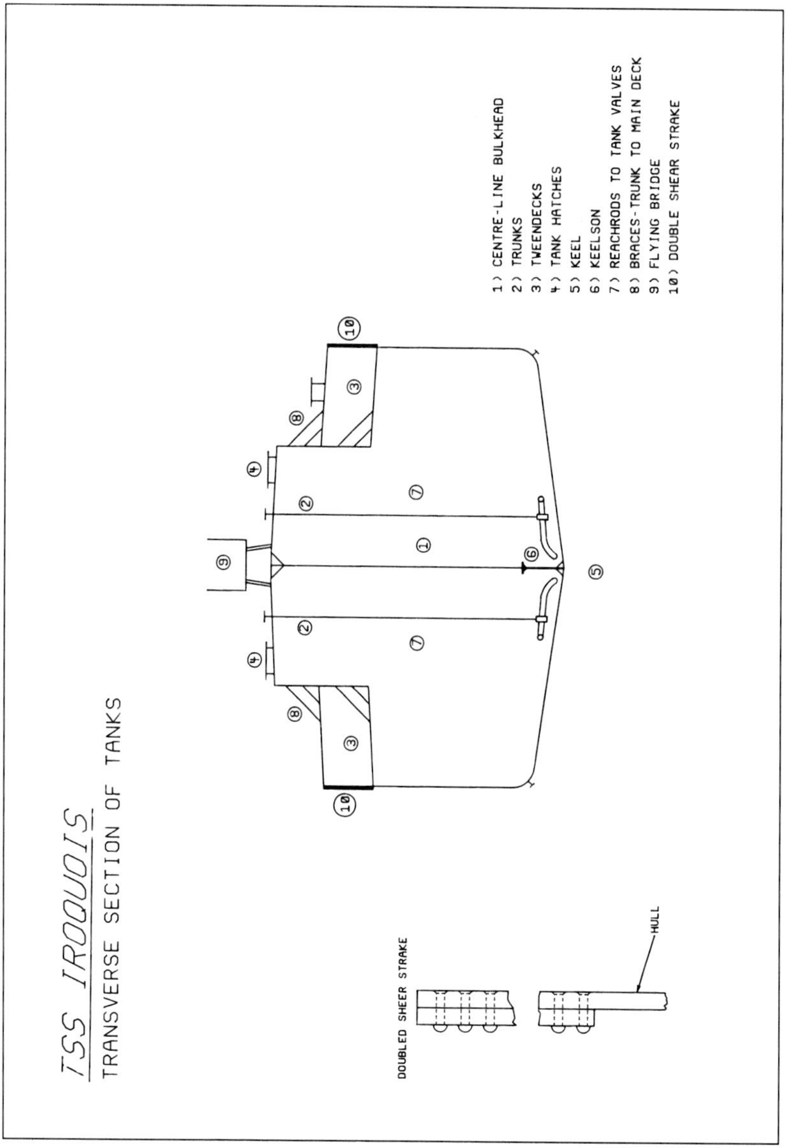
TSS IROQUOIS
TRANSVERSE SECTION OF TANKS
1) CENTRE-LINE BULKHEAD
2) TRUNKS
3) TWEENDECKS
4) TANK HATCHES
5) KEEL
6) KEELSON
7) REACHRODS TO TANK VALVES
8) BRACES-TRUNK TO MAIN DECK
9) FLYING BRIDGE
10) DOUBLE SHEAR STRAKE
DOUBLED SHEER STRAKE
HULL

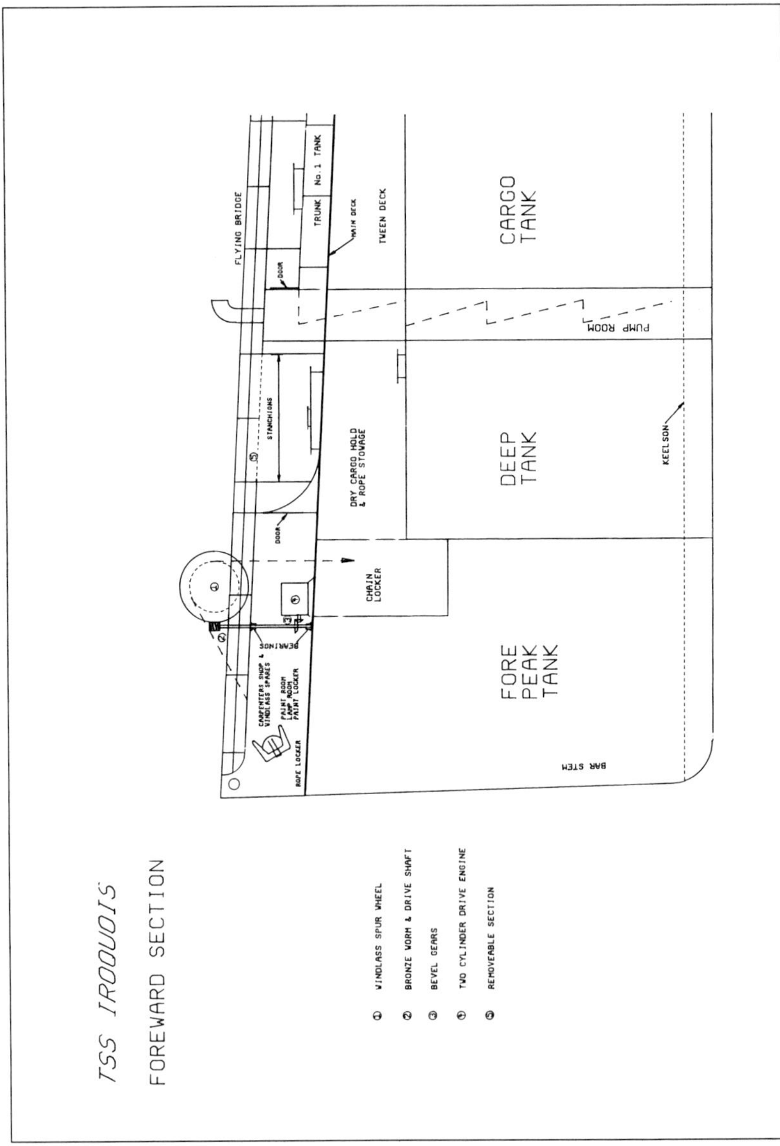
TSS IROQUOIS
FOREWARD SECTION
① WINDLASS SPUR WHEEL
② BRONZE WORM & DRIVE SHAFT
③ BEVEL GEARS
④ TWO CYLINDER DRIVE ENGINE
⑤ REMOVEABLE SECTION
FLYING BRIDGE
TRUNK
No.1 TANK
MAIN DECK
TWEEN DECK
CARGO TANK
DOOR
PUMP ROOM
STANCHIONS
DRY CARGO HOLD & ROPE STOWAGE
DEEP TANK
KEELSON
DOOR
CHAIN LOCKER
BEARINGS
CARPENTERS SHOP & WINDLASS SPARES
PAINT ROOM
LAMP ROOM
PAINT LOCKER
ROPE LOCKER
FORE PEAK TANK
BAR STEM

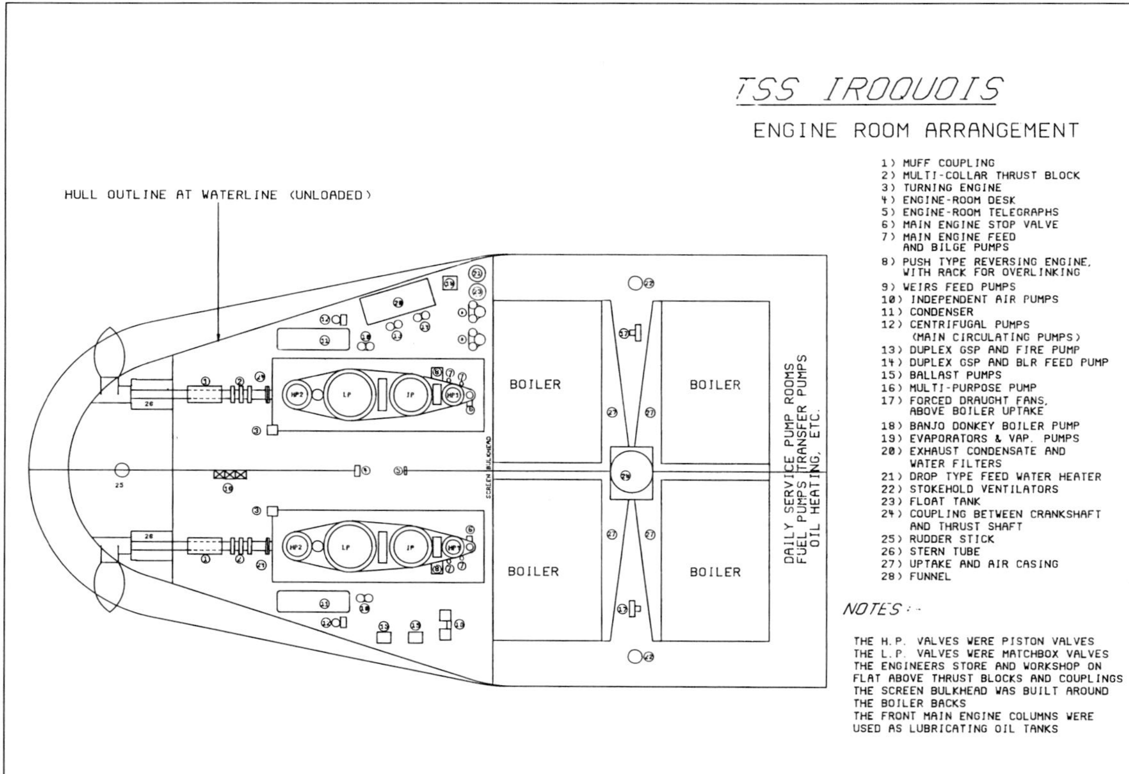
TSS IROQUOIS
ENGINE ROOM ARRANGEMENT
1) MUFF COUPLING
2) MULTI-COLLAR THRUST BLOCK
3) TURNING ENGINE
4) ENGINE-ROOM DESK
5) ENGINE-ROOM TELEGRAPHS
6) MAIN ENGINE STOP VALVE
7) MAIN ENGINE FEED AND BILGE PUMPS
8) PUSH TYPE REVERSING ENGINE, WITH RACK FOR OVERLINKING
9) WEIRS FEED PUMPS
10) INDEPENDENT AIR PUMPS
11) CONDENSER
12) CENTRIFUGAL PUMPS (MAIN CIRCULATING PUMPS)
13) DUPLEX GSP AND FIRE PUMP
14) DUPLEX GSP AND BLR FEED PUMP
15) BALLAST PUMPS
16) MULTI-PURPOSE PUMP
17) FORCED DRAUGHT FANS, ABOVE BOILER UPTAKE
18) BANJO DONKEY BOILER PUMP
19) EVAPORATORS & VAP. PUMPS
20) EXHAUST CONDENSATE AND WATER FILTERS
21) DROP TYPE FEED WATER HEATER
22) STOKEHOLD VENTILATORS
23) FLOAT TANK
24) COUPLING BETWEEN CRANKSHAFT AND THRUST SHAFT
25) RUDDER STICK
26) STERN TUBE
27) UPTAKE AND AIR CASING
28) FUNNEL
NOTES:-
THE H.P. VALVES WERE PISTON VALVES
THE L.P. VALVES WERE MATCHBOX VALVES
THE ENGINEERS STORE AND WORKSHOP ON FLAT ABOVE THRUST BLOCKS AND COUPLINGS
THE SCREEN BULKHEAD WAS BUILT AROUND THE BOILER BACKS
THE FRONT MAIN ENGINE COLUMNS WERE USED AS LUBRICATING OIL TANKS
HULL OUTLINE AT WATERLINE (UNLOADED)
BOILER
BOILER
BOILER
BOILER
DAILY SERVICE PUMP ROOMS
FUEL PUMPS TRANSFER PUMPS
OIL HEATING, ETC.
SCREEN BULKHEAD
HP2
LP
IP
HP1

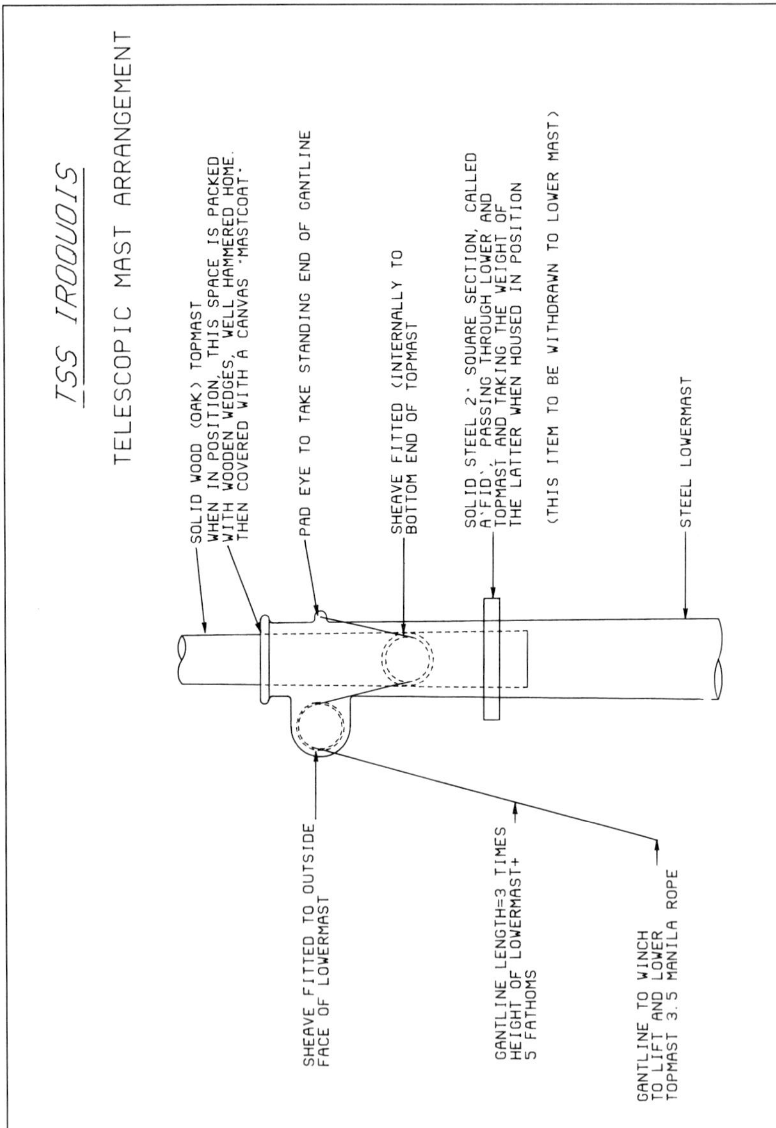
TSS IROQUOIS
TELESCOPIC MAST ARRANGEMENT
SOLID WOOD (OAK) TOPMAST
WHEN IN POSITION, THIS SPACE IS PACKED WITH WOODEN WEDGES, WELL HAMMERED HOME. THEN COVERED WITH A CANVAS 'MASTCOAT'
PAD EYE TO TAKE STANDING END OF GANTLINE
SHEAVE FITTED (INTERNALLY TO BOTTOM END OF TOPMAST
SOLID STEEL 2" SQUARE SECTION, CALLED A'FID', PASSING THROUGH LOWER AND TOPMAST AND TAKING THE WEIGHT OF THE LATTER WHEN HOUSED IN POSITION
(THIS ITEM TO BE WITHDRAWN TO LOWER MAST)
STEEL LOWERMAST
SHEAVE FITTED TO OUTSIDE FACE OF LOWERMAST
GANTLINE LENGTH=3 TIMES HEIGHT OF LOWERMAST+ 5 FATHOMS
GANTLINE TO WINCH TO LIFT AND LOWER TOPMAST 3.5 MANILA ROPE

Iroquois *towing* Navahoe.

*Drop of bad weather 1924.*

*Left and below:*
*Drop of bad weather 1924.*

Iroquois *1913*.

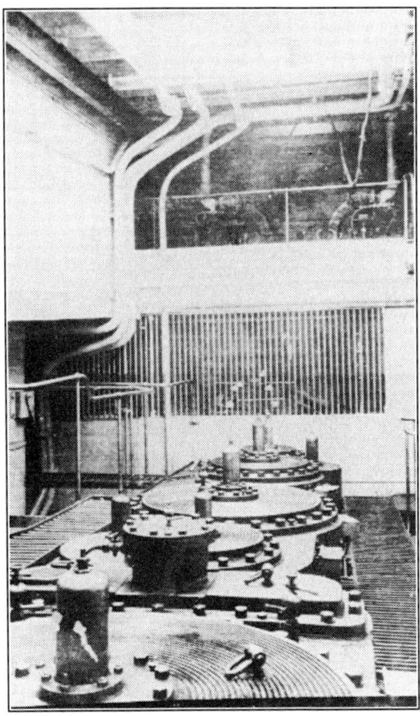

*Possibly the only photo of the engine room of the* Iroquois. *Shows the cylinder heads of starboard engine.*

Iroquois *in dry dock.*

*Left: Painting manmast and shrouds.*
*Below:* Iroquois *off Purfleet.*

Iroquois *at Baytown US Gulf 1928.*

# THE *NAVAHOE*

THE *Navahoe* at 7,718 tons, like the *Iroquois*, was named after a Red Indian tribe, and was also built by Harland and Wolff of Belfast. She was launched on 10 October 1907, by Mrs Powell, and entered service on 3 March 1908. The lines on which the *Navahoe* was built were hardly those of a conventional sailing ship, but she was rigged as a six-masted schooner, often known as a 'bald-headed' schooner, and was at that time the longest sailing vessel in the world. She had a length of 450 feet and a breadth of 58 feet, moulded depth of 33 feet.

She was fitted with a single oil-fired boiler and had engines housed beneath the forecastle head for cargo pumping. The steam produced supplied auxiliaries such as generators and winches for hoisting the sails at each mast. When one considered how large these sails were, it can be understood why it was so necessary to have the winches. Steam also supplied the towing winch. She had a cargo capacity of 9,250 tons contained in eighteen separate compartments to allow for the carrying of mixed cargoes. She had a bunker capacity of 600 tons.

The foremast acted as a funnel for the single boiler. Each of the other masts was hollow, and each was used as a ventilator which helped carry off the gases from the tanks below. She carried sails on all her six masts, although they were rarely hoisted. The masts were: fore; main; mizzen; jigger; spanker; and driver, and the mast of the driver was also used as a funnel for the galley. Each mast was bent afore, and had an aft sail of the strongest storm canvas made (00 gauge). The booms were 65 feet and the gaffs 60 feet in length, and this gave her a total area of sail approaching twenty-eight thousand square feet.

The *Navahoe*, for her size, was considered under-sailed, and when released from her tow made very poor headway, even with a favourable wind, not much more than steerage way. Invariably she went off to leeward.

The ship's company varied between twenty-three and thirty-five and was berthed aft, except the engineers who were all berthed beneath the forecastle head. She had certified accommodation for forty persons. The navigating bridge of the *Navahoe* was strongly built and was very rounded; it was mounted on the forecastle deck immediately in front of the foremast.

It was fitted with large port-holes instead of the large windows. Due to the small amount of freeboard when loaded, heavy seas frequently swept over the forecastle.

The *Navahoe*, like the *Iroquois*, had no bulwarks; instead she had stanchions and chains to act as guards. At the stern there was another deckhouse which had an entrance to the officers' quarters, saloon and steering gear. She had nine tanks on each side, and in the centre of the vessel running from forecastle head to the poop deck was the uppermost part of these tanks, which projected about three feet above the surface of the deck, known as a 'trunk deck'. This part housed the safety valves to each tank that lifted at 5lbs per square inch and discharged fumes given off by the oil cargo.

The rudder of the *Navahoe* was a large one for the size of the ship, and measured 12'6″ from pintles to the extreme edge. The *Navahoe* was steered from the navagation bridge on the forecastle, and the rudder was operated by steam steering gear aft. In those days ships' owners still had doubts about the reliability of steam steering gear, and had an extra steering gear installed. By this means six men, using hand connection, could steer the vessel.

Several times during her career in tow ships came racing up and, seeing her being towed, hoped to get part of a salvage job. They used to ask the captain of the *Iroquois* (Captain Pritchard) how long he had been towing the *Navahoe*, and it was not until he drily replied: 'About twenty years,' that they left him alone.

*Left and below:*
Navahoe, *picking up the tow at close quarters. (Courtesy of Esso.)*

Navahoe.

# THE TOWING GEAR

BECAUSE of the enormous towing strain involved in towing the *Navahoe* it meant that it was impossible to tow with only one hawser, and conventional towing hooks were completely unsuitable. The idea was developed of having two towing engines, that really in effect were two winches.

One was situated on the poop deck of the *Iroquois* and one on the forecastle of the *Navahoe.* One end of each of the two seven-inch cables was made fast on each vessel and the other, or 'free' end ran to the drum of the towing engine. Towing strain was cushioned by steam pressure on the towing engines, where steam was applied at all times. When the strain became greater, during violent pitching in bad weather, the cable would suddenly become taut. This in turn would cause the towing engines to unwind cable against the steam pressure to ease the load. When the load came off the cables the steam pressure would regain control and haul in the slack until the pressure was equalized. The cable used was Bullwant seven-inch towing hawser. The winches coiled away exactly the amount of cable they had previously paid out.

This next part is an extract from Lloyd's List 2/10/1909:

> As the hawser passes from the drum, it passes between two revolving sheaves, so placed, that when hauling in, the tow-rope coils away evenly on the drum and not riding over the other turns. Passing through these sheaves, the hawser is then taken through a patent towing chock in the bows. Should the *Navahoe* take a shear this towing chock revolves, and ensures that there is always a straight pull on the sheave through which the hawser leaves the barge. On the forecastle head of the *Navahoe* are two large towing hooks which could be used if the *Navahoe* was taking the *Iroquois'* hawser instead of using her own. These hooks are of simple construction and the hawser could be released merely by drawing out a steel pin. Fish oil was freely used for the preservation of the towing hawser, and as it was hauled in, it was given a liberal coating of this oil.

The *Navahoe* was usually towed from its berth by tugs to a suitable deep-water place where she anchored to wait for the *Iroquois.* Connecting up the tow was achieved by the *Iroquois* slowing steaming across the *Navahoe's* bows at an angle and dropping a two-inch diameter grass rope with a small buoy attached to it so that it trailed in the wake of the *Iroquois.* Being a grass rope, it floated behind. The crew of the *Navahoe* threw grappling hooks to catch the grass rope, which was then hauled on board. This was followed by a heavy manila rope. It was essential to use this rope as a messenger to enable the heavy towing wire to be hauled on board and made fast. Only then, after much signalling by semaphore or Aldis lamp, could the vessels be drawn together and the second wire passed between the two vessels, and the tow could commence. When they were both under way the cable length was increased. Only on two occasions in their history did a tug deliver the messenger line.

After the *Iroquois* was scrapped the towing wire was used as a river mooring wire for tankers using the Dingle Oil jetty in the River Mersey.

# THE PARTNERSHIP OF THE TWINS

THE skippers of these two ships were usually on good terms with each other, and often took the mickey out of each other by referring to 'my tug boat skipper' or 'my barge skipper'. Largely due to expert seamanship and their elaborate towing gear, they were conspicuously free from accidents during their long partnership. Seaman will readily understand that towing a vessel the size of the *Navahoe* fully laden across the North Atlantic in all weathers, especially in winter gales, was a formidable proposition. Towing was carried out by using two seven-inch steel cables, 600 fathoms long (3,600 feet) although the usual length paid out between the two ships was 475–500 fathoms (3,000 feet). This of course varied with the conditions, and was lengthy in bad weather. With a heavy sea and spray, the *Iroquois* would often lose sight of the *Navahoe.* The towing of the *Navahoe* was a tricky operation in bad weather, and called for constant tow length changes. To accomplish this the wireless was used. The *Navahoe* had a long wireless aerial strung out along the tops of her masts. In those days there was no radio-telephone and only Morse was used.

The two ships were an economical way of transporting oil in bulk, as one set of engines provided the motive power for the transportation of two cargoes. When leaving and entering port the *Iroquois* used to cast off the *Navahoe* which was then manoeuvred by tugs, but once clear of shallow waters the tow was taken up.

The partnership began with a maiden voyage that commenced on 3 March 1908. The two returned to Gravesend on 13 April. The *Iroquois* usually carried about 8,800 tons of refined oil while the *Navahoe* carried about 9,250 tons (usually spirit) from the US Gulf ports (Galveston). The *Iroquois* discharged at Purfleet and the *Navahoe* at Thameshaven. Their future operations were watched with keen interest, not merely from the seamen's point of view, or the marine engineers' point of view, but also from the ships' owners' standpoint of results and finance. Remember that the towing idea was really an experiment.

Between 3 March 1908 and May 1917, the *Iroquois* and the *Navahoe* made one hundred and forty-eight Atlantic crossings, usually between the US

Gulf ports of Baton Rouge and Galveston to London (Purfleet and Thameshaven) at an average speed of 8.7 knots.

It seems a quirk of fate that most of the collisions that the *Navahoe* was involved in were while she was not under the tow of the *Iroquois*. As early as 3 August 1908, the *Navahoe* was in collision with SS *Asama*, a small bunkering tanker, while both vessels were anchored off Staten Island, Quarantine, New York. Both vessels had dragged their anchors. (The *Asama* was a 2,000-ton tanker built in 1897 at Greenock, for J.M. Wood, and was named after a town in Japan.)

In 1909 the *Iroquois* in common with the rest of Anglo-American Oil Co ships was fitted with a wireless.

Extract from Lloyd's List, 1 August 1911:

> St. Pierre (Miquelon). The schooner *Rose L.* of St. Pierre, which arrived here today, had been in collision with steamer *Iroquois* and sustained slight damage.

(The *Rose L.* was a 44-ton schooner built in 1876 at Essex, Mass., USA and owned by F.G. Smith.)

Extract from Lloyd's List:

> Tug *H.B. Moore JR.* of the White Star Towing Co., was struck by the propeller of the British steamer *Iroquois*, from London, about noon on the 29th of November 1911 and sank off the bell buoy, at Thomskinville. Merriott and Chapmans derrick *Century* is raising the wreck.

The *Iroquois* left the UK with the *Navahoe* in tow; both were in ballast. On 16 December 1911, when they were twenty-five miles south-west of the Lizard, the steering gear of the *Navahoe* broke down allowing her rudder to swing free. Various damage was done to the stern-post and after parts of the vessel. As the pair of ships was still under builders' warranty the *Iroquois* towed her first to Falmouth for examination and then on to Harland and Wolff, Belfast, for repairs. It was found necessary to carry out modifications to the steering gear, and she had to dry-dock, for the first time since she was built.

The *Iroquois* continued on to New York solo. On the morning of 21 January 1912, in fog, the *Iroquois* grounded on the Nassau Bar on her way to Charleston. Fortunately she grounded on the incoming tide. After attempting to go astern for some time without making any headway, the engines were stopped and the ship waited for the tide to rise. An hour or so later the tide had risen sufficiently for her to float off, and she continued her journey. On arrival in port she was examined, and it was found she had sustained no damage.

The repairs to the *Navahoe* took so long that it was not until 2 March that the *Iroquois* was able to pick up the *Navahoe* and continue with the partnership. On 12 March 1912, just ten days later, the *Navahoe* and the steamer *City of Savannah* collided in New York harbour after dragging their anchors. Both had their bows badly damaged. The *Navahoe*, when surveyed, was found to have her stem along with sixty bow plates, including frames and stringers, and decks in way, badly damaged. However, this did not prevent her sailing for the UK.

(The *City of Savannah* of 5,654 tons was built in 1907 by Delaware River Co, Chester, Pa., and was operated by the Ocean SS of Savannah.)

On 5 April 1912 the *Narragansett* was in the Nantucket Sound when she had to stop engines and drop anchor, having suffered an engine breakdown. The *Iroquois* tied up alongside and her engineers were able to board the *Narragansett* and give assistance. It was on the return journey to Purfleet that they must have been several hundred miles south of the *Titanic* when she sank on 15 April 1912. It is recorded that the *Iroquois* and *Navahoe* left New York on 8 April and passed the Lizard on 24 April arriving at Southend on 1 May 1912.

By the beginning of 1914, Anglo-American Oil Co was the largest oil-carrying fleet in the world.

On 15 February 1914 the *Navahoe* dragged her anchor in New York harbour and went hard aground, but she managed to float off with the tide and was undamaged.

On 28 June 1914 the First World War started.

Prior to 1916 Anglo-American Oil Co had carried out a lot of research into the advantage of oil-burning boilers. It was found that there were vast economies in oil burning. The decision was taken to convert most of the coal-burning ships to oil burning, provided that there were bunkering facilities on their normal voyage routes. The *Iroquois*' normal run was to New York and the Gulf ports and there were adequate facilities at all of these. In February 1916 the oil-burning equipment was installed as the ship lay in New York harbour, which involved the fitting of new furnace fronts as well as all the fuel pumps, steam heating coils and associated pipe-work. Steam heating coils were needed as the oil could not be pumped in its cold state because it was too viscous. The oil-burning system installed on the *Iroquois* was 'White' Liquid Fuel System. The installation of oil-burning equipment caused many problems with the engineers on watch, as many hours were spent watching the condition of the flames through a little spy-hole on the front of each furnace.

It was vital that the space previously occupied by the coal bunkers was scrupulously clean before they could be used as oil bunkers. The oil bunkers took up much less space than that occupied by coal, and the extra room was used for the oil fuel pumps. The vacant space on the upper deck allowed changes to be made to enlarge the crew accommodation.

The changeover to oil burning actually reduced the cost of fuel per day, but the biggest savings were in manpower. In the days of coal burning ten firemen and seven coal trimmers were carried. After conversion to oil, only six firemen were carried.

Extract from the ship's log book of the SS *Iroquois*, 13 January 1917, while on passage from New York to London:

> Lat 38° 42′ N. Long 46° 52′ W. I hereby certify that at 08.30 I sighted a vessel showing distress signals, altered course and bore down on her, vessel turned out to be the schooner *Molega* of St. Johns, Newfoundland, who was in sinking condition, having sprung a bad leak. Captain Mickenson of the schooner wished to abandon ship, and requested to be taken off. This was done and as the schooner was in the path of vessels, we fired two explosive shells into her, which set her on fire. Noon, bore away on course.

(The *Molega* was a three-masted wooden schooner of 148 tons built in 1882 at Lunenburg, Nova Scotia. She was 91′ 7″ long, 27 ft. wide and had a draught of 8 ft.)

From Lloyd's List, 30 January 1917:

> *Molega* bound for Portugal, crew saved after they had previously taken to the lifeboats and were picked up by the *Iroquois* and the *Navahoe*.

The log book of the *Navahoe* shows a similar entry.

The cargo of the *Molega* had been an interesting one, for amongst it was 250 tons of motor tyres, which had they been salvaged, would have presented a good payout. The captain at that time was a relief skipper and did not feel he should have taken the chance of bringing her in.

From the ship's log of the *Iroquois*, 26 January 1917:

> Downs, at 1.40 am the Norwegian steamer *Barbro* of Christiania dragged her anchor, fell foul of our starboard quarter doing damage to our gunwale bar and several dents and chaffs to shearstrake plate in way of after boats.

(The *Barbro* was a steamer of 2,356 tons built in 1891 at Christiania.)

During the war many of the crew of both ships 'jumped ship' when in New York. America was considered to be the country flowing with milk and honey, and often men would join ship simply as a means of passage to America.

In the days of the reciprocating engines, one of the duties of the watch-keeping engineer was to keep a careful eye on the temperature of the bearings, especially the engine bearings. In particular, the bottom-end bearings were prone to overheating. When one considered that the size of the journal was in the order of about twelve inches in diameter, and the engine would be turning about 80 revolutions per minute, they would be travelling rather fast. It was customary for the engineer to place his hand on the side of the bearing as it was coming down over the top dead centre, to feel the temperature. This was carried out on each side of each bearing in turn. On one occasion, on 3 May 1917, the Assistant Engineer, W.J. Rood's hand jammed on the side of the bearing, probably through wearing a ring, and he was dragged down into the engine. The sump on this type of engine had sloping sides and a gully at the bottom about eighteen inches wide. Luckily, Rood found himself lying in this gulley with the con-rods and bearings whizzing past his body at a frightening speed. The gully was a channel at the bottom used for the collection of oil that had seeped out of the bearings. The engine was shut down, something that can be achieved in seconds on a steam engine, and the engineer was dragged out of the engine. His only injury was a broken finger and a sprained leg. It was said that the shock was so great that his hair turned white in twenty-four hours, and he was placed off duty till the *Iroquois* was passing Deal on the Kent coast where he was put ashore. He was able to rejoin the ship for its next voyage.

In 1917 the 2nd Engineer, Ernest Taphouse, was on the 4–8 watch in the morning. It was the custom on most ships that the engineer's steward would bring down a mug of tea and a slice of toast at about six o'clock. The 2nd Engineer was at the time carrying out some adjustments at the back of one of the main engines, when he spied a slice of toast falling from the top deck of the engine room. A minute later the steward appeared, looked along the length between the engines and, seeing no one, picked up the slice of toast and put it back on the plate. The 2nd Engineer moved round to the front of the engine, where the steward presented him with the tea and toast. 'I'm not eating that toast,' said the 2nd Engineer, 'it's been on the deck!' 'That's alright,' said the steward. 'It didn't fall butter side down.'

The long period of over nine years on this run had to be broken up, as the First World War was at its peak. Stringent convoy systems were in operation (in the latter part of the war) which were not suitable for big ship towing, such as the *Iroquois* and the *Navahoe*. So the two ships were withdrawn in June 1917 and placed on the Texas to Halifax (Nova Scotia) run, where they averaged 10.1 knots, and where they plied between the US Gulf ports of Sabine, Port Arthur and Philadelphia as well as New York and Halifax. On one of these trips they diverted from this route and went up to Halifax where the *Navahoe* discharged her cargo while the *Iroquois* went up the St. Lawrence River to Montreal. In 1917, 3,729,785 tons of Allied shipping had been sunk by the Germans, and in April 1917 U-boats alone had been responsible for sinking 881,000 tons of Allied shipping. This area where they were working was out of the range of the German raiders, and they transported naval oil to Nova Scotia on behalf of the Admiralty. By the end of the war 290,000 tons of oil had been moved by the 'Twins' for the Admiralty in just over fourteen months.

In November 1918, when the war ended, they both returned to their original Gulf to London run until 1930, but before this they both dry-docked at Plymouth.

From Lloyd's List 30/6/1919:

> Dutch auxiliary vessel *Jantje* returned here 28th of June 1919, with damage to port bow above water-line having been in collision at 4 a.m. 28th of June with barge *Navahoe*, anchored off Thameshaven. Latter vessel reported uninjured.

(The *Jantje* was a 190-ton auxiliary schooner cutter built in 1909 by Gebr. Nieestern, Delfzijl and owned by J. Koopman, registered in Groningen. Her dimensions were 97′ 3″ long, 19′ 6″ wide and 6′ 6″ deep.)

From Lloyd's List 24/11/1919:

> Maasslius, 24/11/1919. Tank barge *Navahoe* grounded on the evening of 22nd of November between red buoys No.1 and 2. Floated off yesterday morning with assistance of five tugs, and was towed to Rotterdam.

On this occasion, the 'Twins' had parted company just off Dover. The *Iroquois* went into Thameshaven, discharged part of her cargo and discharged the rest at Cuxhaven. The *Navahoe* was towed to Rotterdam to discharge hers.

On the next trip they encountered a gale that was so strong that one of the towing cables parted and the shoe that was placed underneath the remaining cable had come out. The Captain. (S.W. Smith of *Cutty Sark* fame) ordered the shoe to be replaced by the bosun and his party. They had just completed the job when a huge wave swept over the forecastle, sweeping the whole gang aft down to the tank tops. When they managed to regain shelter it was found that one man was missing and feared overboard. A few minutes later a cry for help was heard and the man was found hanging over the side of the *Navahoe* held fast by a life-line. He was badly injured with a broken thigh. The Captain called for splints and reset the broken limb himself. When he went into hospital on arrival in New York, the hospital stated that they could not have done a better job themselves. The 'Twins' arrived in New York in sub-zero conditions, with all the rigging festooned with icicles. This voyage to New York had taken nineteen days due to the weather.

(Captain S.W. Smith was a renowned captain, who had at one time served as a 2nd Officer of the *Cutty Sark*. He had been imprisoned for manslaughter for having killed a mutineer with a blow from a marlin spike, when he had been a mate in sail. In doing so he had had his Master's Certificate cancelled. After completing the necessary qualifying period he sat the exam again and obtained another Master's Certificate. He died in 1924.)

On 22 March 1920 the *Iroquois* was in collision with the steamer *Rock Island Bridge*, eight miles SSE of the Lizard, while on passage from Antwerp. The *Rock Island Bridge* was very low in water and was towed by steamer *Kenosha* and brought to the mouth of the Helford River, Falmouth, where she was beached. She was subsequently scrapped as a result of the damage she sustained in this collision. The *Iroquois* docked at Purfleet on 24 March with damage to the port bow above the waterline, hawse pipe broken and loss of port anchor. The *Navahoe*, loaded with benzine, had also collided with the *Rock Island Bridge* but did not sustain any damage.

(The *Rock Island Bridge* was a 3,545-ton cable-laying steamer built in 1920 in Newark, New Jersey, by Submarine Boat Corp. and owned by All Seas Marine and Salvage Co Ltd.)

Leaving Baton Rouge on 21 November 1920 and passing New Orleans on the 23rd, the *Iroquois* and the *Navahoe* met bad weather and followed the Norfolk coastline going northwards towards New York. As they were beginning to pass Cape Hatteras they encountered a heavy south-west gale. Three-quarters of a mile of hawser was paid out to ease the strain. The tow still parted and great difficulty was experienced in connecting up, and even when connected the tow parted again. This time it could only be achieved by the *Iroquois* floating oil downstream with a lifebelt and a messenger line attached, but it was many hours before the two were on their way again at reduced speed.

*Painting of the storm off Cape Hatteras showing the* Iroquois *and the* Navahoe *adrift. (Painting by Frank H. Mason, Courtesy of Esso.)*

Cape Hatteras is well known for its bad weather. It is the meeting point of the cold North Atlantic winds and the warm air that blows with the Gulf Stream. When the two meet they often result in violent weather.

In January 1921 the *Iroquois* put into Rotterdam for extensive modifications to be made. A competitive price had been tendered by the Dutch for these changes. An extra bridge was to be added midships as it was difficult for bridge officers to view the *Navahoe*. If the reader compares the photo taken in 1913 with the later ones, the difference in bridges is quite noticeable. She left Rotterdam on 10 May.

Another year passed before the *Navahoe* was involved again, and on 1 June 1921 she was in collision with SS *Silvertown*, a bunkering hulk belonging to Anglo-American Oil Co that was based in Southampton Water, where she suffered damage to her plating, Believe it or not, the *Iroquois* had collided with the *Silvertown* the previous month in the same area! The *Silvertown* stayed at Hamble Spit until September 1924, when she was moved to Algiers and used as a fuel depot ship.

(The *Silvertown* was a tanker of 3,308 tons built in 1873 at Newcastle, owned and operated by Anglo-American Oil Co and named after an East London town.)

The *Navahoe* ran aground in the Port Arthur channel on 9 October 1921, and had to be assisted off by tugs.

It was customary for the *Iroquois* to dry-dock each year, usually at Smiths Dock, North Shields. On one such occasion, in August 1926, the 'Twins' were photographed in dry docks next to each other. On some occasions when Smiths Dock was unable to accommodate them, they dry-docked at Falmouth with Green and Silley Weirs.

On 10 May 1922 there were dockyard strikes all over England, so the 'Twins' went to Rotterdam to dry-dock and carry out repairs. At this point the two parted company; the *Navahoe* went into Thameshaven and on to Schiedam and from there to Rotterdam. These repairs were extensive and they did not leave Rotterdam until 12 June. From there they sailed to Colon, arriving there in ballast, and thence through the Panama Canal westwards, something the *Iroquois* was only to repeat once again in World War II. Towing the *Navahoe* in such a confined space would have been hazardous, and both of them were towed through the canal separately. They journeyed on to San Francisco, arriving on 17 July, where they were to load a cargo of aviation spirit. The time spent in San Francisco was considerable, as it was found that when the spirit was pumped into the cargo tanks of the *Iroquois*, it became discoloured. Although the tanks had been thoroughly cleaned and had previously been used for the carriage of petroleum, there were minute traces of crude oil which were leading to the discolouration. Geoff Dawson states that gangs of Italians, who were all dressed identically, were put on board to carry out the tank cleaning. The *Navahoe* took on a cargo of crude oil and they finally left San Francisco on 5 September, back through the Panama, arriving at Thameshaven on 6 October, where the *Navahoe* discharged all her cargo and the *Iroquois* part of hers. The *Iroquois* travelled on to Hull with the remainder of her cargo and on to North Shields where she dry-docked yet again. She picked up the *Navahoe* on tow again on 1 November.

The 'Twins' docked at Nieuwe Waterweg (Holland) on 6 September 1923 with a cargo of aviation spirit. This was discharged, and the 'Twins' departed for the US Gulf ports, only to be recalled after passing Dover on the 22nd back to Nieuwe Waterweg, where they were both reloaded with their original cargoes. Apparently the aviation spirit had been contaminated by the tanks in which it had been carried, and both cargoes had been refused when the contamination had been found. For once the westbound voyage was made not in ballast, but with full cargoes, to Sabine where the spirit was re-refined.

1924 was a bad year for weather at sea. The *Iroquois'* apprentice, Geoff Dawson, said that the weather was so bad on 8 January that they were hove to for thirty hours and that he experienced the worst weather on that day that he had ever seen; even some of the crew broke down and prayed for deliverance. One of the problems encountered was when the steering gear broke down. Apparently the engine driving the worm that was connected to the steering quadrant moved, resulting in the quadrant being disconnected from the steering. When the ship stopped, the rudder swung round on its stock. The engineers turned to and the engine was put back to its original position. The master and the 2nd and 3rd Mates had to keep continuous watch on the bridge while the Chief Engineer and the 1st Mate struggled to ease the strain on the towing machine as it roared in and out as the wire was torn out and recovered. He described it as a very hairy do, and most of the crew congregated in the forecastle. The weather was bad enough to put the *Iroquois* into dry dock. It was found necessary to renew five plates around the centre section of the ship.

Many years later the Chief Engineer, Ernest Taphouse, related the story of this storm to his family. He graphically described the height of the waves as often being so great that they passed over the funnel, and how he insisted on travelling from the engineers' quarters aft to the midships saloon, where he would take his meals. When asked what happened if a big wave came along when you were halfway along the flying bridge, 'You got wet,' was his reply. 'What did you hang on to?' was the next question. 'Anything,' came the curt reply.

Both ships had their share of mishaps, beginning with the loss of the *Iroquois'* anchor at Jarrow Slake, Newcastle, on 24 January 1924. Her anchor had fouled the moorings of the west buoy deep-water berth. The anchor was slipped at the fifteen-fathom shackle. Three days later on 27 January the anchor of the *Navahoe* fouled the same moorings. The cable parted and she lost her port anchor; part of her cable was lost in the river.

On 8 March the *Navahoe* collided with the tug *Dalzellite* while leaving Sandy Hook Bay, New York Harbour. The tug's stern was damaged. (The *Dalzellite* was a wooden tug of 176 tons built in 1920 by Dachel Carter Boat Company, Beuton Harbour, Michigan. She was owned by Dalzell Towing Co. All this company's tugs were of wooden construction. Her dimensions were 94′ 8″ long, 24′ wide and 14′ 6″ deep.)

On 19 August 1924 the *Iroquois* struck the bank in the South Pass, River Mississippi with her starboard quarter. In doing this she lost three blades from the starboard propeller, and her starboard tailshaft was badly bent, necessitating a replacement, and this entailed dry-docking, in the floating dry dock at New Orleans. Before this could be done she transferred all her cargo of petroleum to the *Navahoe*. At that time there was a Shipyard Union strike, and as a consequence a spare tailshaft had to be fitted by the ship's crew. Does the reader really appreciate the difficulties involved in changing a tailshaft?

Most modern-day tankers have a short intermediate shaft between the engine and the tailshaft. Once this is removed the tailshaft can be withdrawn inboard. The *Iroquois*, remember, was one of the early ships built with engines aft, and in consequence *very* aft, with no intermediate shaft. Because of this, the tailshaft connected directly to the engine crankshaft by means of a large split Muff coupling made from cast iron, probably somewhere in the order of twenty-four inches diameter and probably thirty inches long.

While this was being split and removed another gang was working on the outside removing the boss and what was left of the starboard propeller. Only then could the tailshaft be withdrawn to the outside.

Modern-day ships carry their spare propeller bolted down to the deck; the *Iroquois* carried hers on the deck in the same way. Modern-day ships rarely carry a spare tailshaft, as there is little call for such in an emergency. Spare tailshafts are usually stocked by the company that usually does the repairs. The *Iroquois'* tailshaft was stored in the deep bowels of the engine room, together with two spare propeller blades. To raise the tailshaft to deck level was a mammoth task using chain blocks, guiding it upwards through the engine skylights by using snatch-blocks. Once it reached deck level the dockside cranes took over and lowered it down into the dry dock.

Remember that the old tailshaft and propeller then had to be taken back on board for shipment back to the UK. There are some doubts, of course, as to whether the old tailshaft was taken back to the engine room. The damage was caused when leaving the river to proceed through one of the navigable channels through the delta in to the sea. The main river is very wide and the delta channel quite narrow. The man at the wheel lost control and the stern swung in furiously and struck the bank at Baton Rouge.

On 14 July that year the German MV *Prometheus* of 9,262 tons at lat.31° 36′N.59° 52′W (260 miles east of Bermuda) reported that she was in distress after being disabled by a fire. Steamer *Inverarder* was standing by to give assistance. She was towed into New York by the steamer *Benjamin Brewster* and then by tugs for surveying and reached there on 24 July. After the survey, on 4 September, it was decided that she should be towed to Germany for permanent repairs. The 'Twins' were in New Orleans at that time. The *Navahoe* was left there so that the *Iroquois* could make a more lucrative crossing across the Atlantic to Hamburg with the *Prometheus* in tow. Even this caused some excitement: three or four days after leaving New York the *Prometheus'* steering gear broke down and she took on an uncontrollable shear. This was so bad that it stripped all the towing wire off the towing machine, which had previously been connected to the shackle on her anchor cable. The *Iroquois* had a used spare that was stowed in the forepeak. This was put into service. To do this a rope messenger was passed from the *Iroquois* to the *Prometheus*, but even this got carried away to the extent that the towing wire started to run away. The brake had not been put on, and in the scramble the wire took charge and finished up on the floor of the Great Banks. The *Iroquois* towed the *Prometheus* all the way to Hamburg where they arrived on 29 September, and the *Prometheus'* cargo was discharged. The *Prometheus* was then towed by tugs to Kiel for repairs, where she arrived on 6 October. During a trial run on 23 January 1925 after these repairs, the *Prometheus* ran aground at Hotternan, and she had to put back into Kiel where further repairs took place. However, she was back in service on 26 January. The voyage had been insured separately, and a considerable amount of money was placed on the London market for the towing risk.

At the outbreak of World War II, most German vessels that arrived in American ports had their German crews replaced by Americans. The *Prometheus* was the last German ship to undergo a crew change, and her

Prometheus.
*(Reproduced by permission of the Deutschen Schiffahrtsmuseums, Bremerhaven.)*

Doralia. *(Reproduced by permission of A. Duncan.)*

crew remained on board till 1 April 1940, when an American crew took charge at St. Vincent, Cape Verde Islands, off the West African coast. The *Prometheus*, once taken over by the Americans, was placed on the east coast, and ran between Cristobal, Curacao and Aruba to New York and Baytown via Guantanamo Bay. The *Prometheus* survived the war.

(The *Prometheus* was a motor vessel built in 1923 in Kiel, Germany, registered at Hamburg and belonged to Hamburg Shipping Co. Named after one of the Greek gods.)

When the *Iroquois* got back to the UK on 25 September she was in collision with the tug SS *Doralia* at Long Reach, River Thames, (approach to Purfleet) when her Master misjudged dropping in under the bow of the *Iroquois* to take the head rope for berthing at Purfleet. Geoff Dawson was at the wheel at the time. Some of the *Iroquois'* plates were dented.

(The *Doralia* was a 155-ton tug built in 1914 at South Shields, registered in London and operated by Pattisons till 1934, then by United Steam Tug Co till 1937. From then onwards she was operated by J.S. Watkins. In 1938 her name was changed to *Napia.* At the beginning of December 1939 she was requisitioned for HMS and used for examination purposes. On 20 December 1939 she hit a mine off Ramsgate and was lost with all eight hands.)

On 9 October the same year the *Navahoe* ran aground in the Port Arthur channel inward bound for New Orleans. She was towed off by tugs.

On 26 October the *Iroquois* met mountainous seas on her passage and reported slight deck damage.

Two months later, on 16 December 1925, while inward bound, the *Iroquois* ran aground in the River Mississippi, at Baton Rouge, near New Orleans. Her starboard propeller blades were damaged and she had some damage to her plating. She managed to get off without any assistance.

By the end of 1925 the *Iroquois* had towed the *Navahoe* for over seventeen years and a distance of 686,329 miles at sea, and 42,832 miles on rivers and canals.

One of the 2nd Mates that served on the *Iroquois* in 1925 was a rather difficult character, somewhat bombastic, and unpopular with the rest of the ship's company. This 2nd Mate gave instructions to the ship's carpenter (a very quiet-natured man) to build for him a seaman's chest 30″ × 30″ × 48″. The chest was duly built. When it was completed the 2nd Mate had it filled with ship's stores and the lid firmly screwed down. On arrival in port and in the quiet of the evening, the 2nd Mate asked the carpenter for the keys to his workshop with the intention of removing the chest. The 2nd Mate was never able to sell the contents of the chest, as the workshop doors were only 28″ wide, and the carpenter *had* made the chest to the 2nd Mate's instructions.

Another year went past before either of them were in trouble again, and when it did come, it was double trouble. On 4 September 1926, the *Iroquois* and the *Navahoe* were in collision with each other at the mouth of the River Mississippi at New Orleans, when the *Navahoe* struck the *Iroquois* amidships. This collision caused damage to No. 8 port-side tank which was carrying naphtha. The cargo from this tank was pumped into the fore-peak tank, and the crew carried out temporary repairs. The *Navahoe* had her stem twisted and stem bar fractured, and pumps were used to control the leaks in the fore-peak tanks. The stem bar fracture was temporarily repaired by encasing the damaged area in cement. These repairs were in fact so good that they were left for two years before permanent repairs were carried out.

On 6 January 1928 the *Navahoe* was in collision with the *West Modus* while being manoeuvred in the Houston Channel. Both vessels were slightly damaged.

The wisdom that Chief Engineers sometimes displayed was occasionally similar to that of King Solomon. In 1929, some time after having left the UK, one of the firemen knocked at the Chief Engineer's cabin door. He told the Chief that he had something important to tell him. Apparently he had been carrying a cloth bag containing ⅝″ nuts and bolts, and had unfortunately tripped. The bag had opened, and the nuts and bolts had fallen into one of the engines. The Chief asked the fireman to show him exactly where the nuts and bolts had fallen. They had not actually fallen into the engine, but into the pump mechanism of the port engine. There was a potential danger of irreversible damage to the air pump if they were not removed.

It was possible to run the main engine without the air pump but this would have posed quite a few problems. Being a twin-screw vessel the voyage could continue on one engine, even though they were towing the *Navahoe*. The Chief left the engine-room to inform the Captain that in his opinion it would be better to shut down the port engine and remove the offending nuts and bolts.

The port engine was duly shut down and the air pump stripped, cleared and reassembled. This must have made the Chief Engineer rather unpopular, as he turned-to even the off-watch engineers to carry out this work. When all was completed, the Chief once again began the long journey back to the Captain's cabin to let him know that the engine was ready to put back into service. (This was just a courtesy.) The Captain told the Chief that he should give the stoker a good dressing-down and log him a half-day's pay. The Chief replied that if something similar ever happened again to the fireman or anyone else on the ship, they would be far too scared to tell. Indeed, he said, he would be far more inclined to thank the fireman for informing him about the accident.

On 17 March 1930, while the *Navahoe* was being towed to the Thameshaven jetty, she collided with the French tank steamer *Melpomene* which was at anchor. The *Navahoe* was damaged on her port bow above the water-line and the *Melpomene* had damage to her starboard bow above the water-line.

(The *Melpomene* was a tanker of 7,011 tons, built in Bordeaux in 1923, and named after the Greek Muse of tragedy.)

The Chief Engineer on board a ship never actually stands a watch but is effectively on call at all times. One time in 1930 he was called to the engine-room by the 3rd Engineer, who reported that one of the stern glands was leaking badly. The two ships had been passing through a particularly bad storm, and it was normal for the glands to leak slightly. The usual remedy was to tighten up each nut (there were six nuts around each gland) about a quarter of a turn until the leakage abated. The four top nuts were easily accessible; the lower two necessitated climbing into the bilge and crouching down in order to tighten them.

The 2nd Engineer, who had been on the previous watch, had only tightened the four upper nuts and had not bothered with the lower ones, and had not tightened them equally, and in doing so had sheared off two of the studs. He had been under the influence of drink prior to going on watch, and as a result had a couldn't-care-less attitude. The Chief Engineer turned out all the engineers to make repairs. They had to drill out the remains of the old studs with post drills and ratchets. This was no easy feat in the days before portable electric drills, and the holes had to be re-tapped. The work was carried out while there was a high sea running. The Chief Engineer was at that particular time the only engineer on board who was able to use a lathe, and it was he who produced new studs. (The lathe was treadle operated.)

When all had been completed he thanked the engineers for the assistance that they had given and returned to his cabin. The 2nd Engineer was summoned and informed that he was sacked and that he would be put ashore at the next port of call and signed off with a D.R. (decline to report). He would be given a passage home by another of the company's vessels. For the rest of the voyage the Chief Engineer took over his watch.

For a short while in 1930 the *Iroquois* was laid up off Southend. On 19 July a squall blew up and it was so strong that the *Iroquois* started dragging

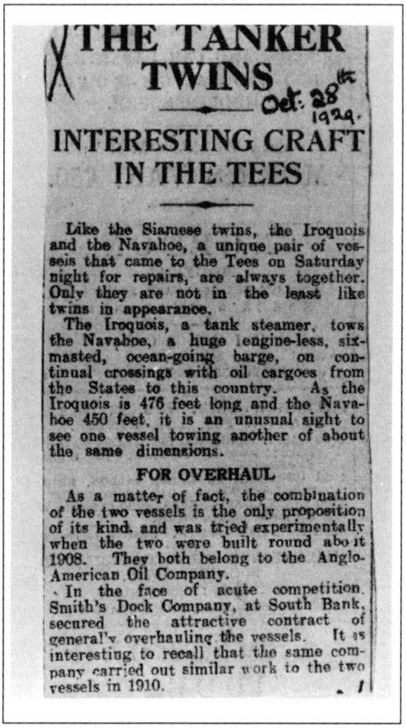

THE TANKER TWINS

Oct. 28th 1929.

INTERESTING CRAFT IN THE TEES

Like the Siamese twins, the Iroquois and the Navahoe, a unique pair of vessels that came to the Tees on Saturday night for repairs, are always together. Only they are not in the least like twins in appearance.

The Iroquois, a tank steamer, tows the Navahoe, a huge engine-less, six-masted, ocean-going barge, on continual crossings with oil cargoes from the States to this country. As the Iroquois is 476 feet long and the Navahoe 450 feet, it is an unusual sight to see one vessel towing another of about the same dimensions.

FOR OVERHAUL

As a matter of fact, the combination of the two vessels is the only proposition of its kind, and was tried experimentally when the two were built round about 1908. They both belong to the Anglo-American Oil Company.

In the face of acute competition, Smith's Dock Company, at South Bank, secured the attractive contract of generally overhauling the vessels. It is interesting to recall that the same company carried out similar work to the two vessels in 1910.

*Newspaper article, 28/10/29.*

its anchor. As there were other vessels anchored in the vicinity, this was a perilous position to be in. As the bows swung round there was a thump as the bows of another ship, the SS *Urla*, collided with the *Iroquois*. When the crew of the *Iroquois* looked over the side of the bow they could see a large dent in the ship's side just below the fifth porthole along. The dent was about two inches deep, and the ship's side-plate was about an inch thick. It was decided to carry out an internal inspection to make sure there were no fractures. The cabins were searched without finding any dents. The cabin with the fifth porthole contained a man fast asleep on his bunk, which was outboard. It was assumed that this could not have been the cabin that had been dented, because the man would have woken up. So the cabins were searched to no avail. It was decided that the sleeping man's cabin was the only possible one for the dent. They moved the man's head away from the ship's side and there was the two-inch dent in inch-thick steel. That man slept soundly! (The SS *Urla* was a 5,198-ton steamer, built at Ardrossan in 1924 and belonged to Bowrings.)

From 21 July to 18 August 1930 the 'Twins' dry-docked at Shields and this was the last time that they were ever to dry-dock at the same time. Never again were they to grace the Tyne with their presence.

# THE PARTING OF THE WAYS

By 1930 the *Navahoe* was over twenty years old. This was considered quite old for a ship that had been used for the transportation of spirit continually. By this time the thickness of the tanks and plating had degenerated to such an extent that she could not meet the safety requirements required by Lloyd's Registry for sailing vessels. Spirit carriers degenerated at a faster rate than crude or refined oil carriers. August 24th 1930 found the *Iroquois* towing the *Navahoe* for its last transatlantic voyage, arriving in New Orleans on 17 September. This was the parting of the ways. The *Iroquois* loaded and returned to Purfleet and the *Navahoe* turned south and was towed by tugs to Cristobel and delivered into Venezuelan owners' hands. The *Navahoe* was then towed to the mouth of the San Juan river in Venezuela, sold to the Creole Petroleum Corporation (a Standard Oil subsidary company) and used as a floating storage hulk. She was stationed at the Maturin Bar.

Most modern tankers at that time were too deep-draughted to take on a full cargo at the oil terminal at Caripito, sixty miles up the river. They topped up their cargo from the *Navahoe*, from its 90,000-barrel storage hulk, after they had passed over the bar, and before they proceeded on their voyage. The *Navahoe* served in this capacity for a further six years until there was an improvement in local loading conditions: probably a dredged channel put her out of business. She was taken in tow for the last time on 27 June 1936 and was ceremoniously scuttled in a predetermined position fifty miles north of Dragons Mouth, Trinidad. Obviously this was considered a cheaper proposition than towing her to a ship-breakers.

By the time 1930 arrived the *Iroquois* and the *Navahoe* had been in partnership for over twenty-two years and had, in those years covered some 1,044,161 sea miles. It really was a marvellous feat, and it seems incredible that in all that time the towing hawsers only parted once. This, really, is a tribute to the seamanship of the officers and crew that manned both vessels.

# THOSE ACCIDENTS

THE previous pages gave a factual account of the *Iroquois* and the *Navahoe*. The information has been gleaned from many sources. I advertised in the *Sea Breezes* and other nautical magazines, and I was amazed at some of the replies that I received, notably the ones from Geoff Dawson, who is mentioned on several occasions. The ship's logs and voyage record cards gave some help as well as Lloyd's List and Lloyd's Weekly Casualty Reports. The wartime escapades of the *Iroquois* were mainly gleaned from the Admiralty convoy and damage reports and personal experiences of those who sailed on the *Iroquois*.

Many readers will wonder why it was that the *Iroquois* and the *Navahoe* were frequently aground in the area around Baton Rouge. The only references in these accounts were gained from Lloyd's Weekly Casualty Reports, but the reader can be assured that there were many more occasions that were not mentioned and only show on the Voyage Record Cards. These were *not* caused by bad seamanship. The River Mississippi has a delta that has several channels that are navigable. In the days prior to the 1930s these channels were not kept dredged clear. In consequence, if a ship lost, say its anchor, in one of the channels, a bank of silt would built up by the small restriction caused by the anchor.

Spring tides and neap tides, as well as bad weather, would often have a tendency to move the banks away from the marked channels, thus causing many ships to run aground. Any voyage record card of ships that traded regularly in that area at that time would show a large number of groundings.

Running aground at low tide or when the tide was on its ebb, did not normally present much of a problem, except possible damage to the bottom plates of the hull as on occasions they were damaged. The normal practice was to anchor and wait for the tide to rise sufficiently for her to float off. Grounding at high tide invariably required the assistance of tugs. However, the men of the *Iroquois* were men of intuition. When she was grounded beneath the bows, the forepeak tank that contained fresh water was pumped overboard to lighten the ship forward. If this measure did not allow the ship to move astern and into deeper water, then part of the cargo from the forward holds was simply pumped into the after holds.

Another method of lightening the ship was to lower the anchor and cable, and draw off the grounded part and then pull up the anchor again.

On occasions the *Iroquois* grounded on one side of the vessel. This was a simple matter to overcome. The *Iroquois* had summer tanks that were in fact 'tween decks but were never used for carrying cargo. The cargo from the side that was grounded was pumped into the tanks on the other side that were only partly filled. This process was known as 'tipping'. When she was clear of the grounding it was pumped back to maintain the trim.

(The 'tween decks of the *Iroquois* were mainly used for stowage of the towing gear, wires, shackles and blocks, etc. The steering rods from the bridge to the poop ran overhead through the starboard 'tween deck. Under loaded conditions, especially during heavy weather, this gear had to be lubricated from within the 'tween deck. The 'tween decks ran the whole length of the ship and had access from the engine-room.)

Readers may think that the *Iroquois* and the *Navahoe* were involved in a lot of collisions, again *not* through bad seamanship. Towing a large vessel like the *Navahoe* was no easy task. A strong wind would push the *Navahoe* to one side, causing her to shear; this would inevitably cause problems steering the *Iroquois*. If the reader still believes that they had a lot of collisions, try looking up in Lloyd's Weekly Casualty Reports, years 1920–1925, the escapades of the *Corncrake*, a small vessel owned by General Steam Navigation Co.

The voyage record cards were compiled by the Captains of each ship from 1927 onwards, but voyages were always recorded by Lloyd's. I have used the same format and copied thereon, so that the reader can trace the dates of arrival and departure of ports of call as well as incidents.

The *Iroquois'* usual port of call in the UK was Purfleet. However, Geoff Dawson tells me that Anglo-American Oil Co were very crafty in their dealings on some occasions. Sometimes they docked at Southampton where the Fawley refinery is situated. The cargo was pumped out of *Iroquois* and into a tank, and immediately pumped back into the *Iroquois* when she delivered it as part cargoes to places like Nykobing and Copenhagen in Denmark and Gothenberg in Sweden. By the time it was delivered to these ports, believe it or not, it was considered a British export.

The carrying of the different cargoes was in different ways quite dangerous. Benzine, now considered as an aromatic hydrocarbon, though not very volatile, has a boiling point of only 80 degrees C. It is very toxic and is carcinomatous. Naphtha is a particular 'cut' of petroleum and is now used in the processing industry where many substances are extracted from it. It is one of the most dangerous cargoes and is highly carcinomatous. In those days it was used as a heating and lighting fuel. Petroleum is again another 'cut' and is a crude natural mixture, and another dangerous cargo.

# AFTER THE PARTNERSHIP

THE *Iroquois* continued to run solo from 1930 and occasionally took special assignments in her stride. One of these took place on 5 September 1930 when she towed the Anglo-American Oil Co MV *Narragansett* of 6,899 tons, up the river to New Orleans, after she had broken the crankshaft on her starboard engine. The *Iroquois* took her in tow on 20 September and the pair of them arrived off Southend on 9 October. Towing a large vessel like the *Narragansett*, which was loaded with benzine, in confined waters such as the Thames would have been hazardous for both vessels, so the *Narragansett* was towed to Shellhaven where her cargo was discharged. A week later she had been towed by tugs and docked in North Shields on the Tyne. Because of the complexity of her repairs she did not leave Shields till 15 December.

It seems the *Narragansett* was doomed to crankshaft failures. On 29 August 1925 she had had to dock with two crankshaft webs cracked, and had sailed for Manchester and made it home on only one engine.

The *Narragansett* was the first Anglo-American ocean-going motor ship and had been built in 1920.

The *Iroquois* (in common with a quarter of the world's tanker fleet) was laid up off Southend, in the Thames estuary, from 11 January 1931 for just over a year. During this time the only people left on board were the Captain, Chief Engineer, donkey-man, cook and two deck-hands. Those that were engine room staff had to grease and oil the engines daily as well as giving the engines a quarter of a turn a day, to prevent the formation of rust in the cylinders. These great big engines, which were over twenty feet high, had to be turned by hand. It has to be appreciated by the reader that there was a turning gear at the after end of each engine. This was operated by two men pulling on a long arm about six feet long with a ratchet on it that turned the engine.

On 22 February 1932 an Anglo-American Oil Company tanker, MV *Cheyenne* of 8,825 tons, at lat.36° 48′ N long. 640° 48′ W, lost one of the blades from its single propeller. The blades were of the bolt-on type that bolted on to a central boss, and the bolts had sheared off. The *Cheyenne* radioed to other company ships telling them of her plight, and stated that she was proceeding at a reduced speed of eight knots due to the vibration. On 2 March the *Cheyenne* radioed to say that her engineers on board believed that another of the propeller blades was coming loose. The *Cheyenne* stopped engines when she was about 1,400 miles from Land's End.

The message was picked up by the MV *Chesapeake* (8,955 tons, and built in 1928; another Anglo-American Oil Company vessel) who was only a hundred miles away from the *Cheyenne*. She asked the *Chesapeake* to come closer and stand by. With high seas running the skipper brought the *Chesapeake* to within fifty yards of the *Cheyenne*, and rockets with heaving lines were fired by the Second Mate. On the second attempt he was successful. To the heaving line was attached a messenger line which in turn took the cable that was to do the towing. This was done with great difficulty and took about two hours.

The skipper of the *Chesapeake* was inexperienced at towing and instead of working up speed gradually, ordered half ahead. Up came the tow wire out of the water and would have become taut and probably have snapped. The day was saved by the quick intervention of the Second Mate who rang down for dead slow ahead and then gently worked up to a reasonable towing speed. The Second Mate, Geoffrey Dawson, had served for several years on the *Iroquois* and was of course conversant with the skill of towing large vessels.

March 3rd came and the *Chesapeake* started towing the *Cheyenne* from a position lat.46° 43′ N long.36° 58′ W. The *Chesapeake* and the *Cheyenne* were only equipped with mooring wires and not towing cables.

The *Cheyenne* had to start her engines and run at about 55 r.p.m. (4–5 knots) to reduce the strain on the tow due to the heavy weather that they were encountering. (Winter North Atlantic has very fierce gales, and high seas.) However, by 5 March they had worked up to a speed of 7.5 knots and by 7 March they had reached a position of lat.49° 18′ N and long.21° 6′ W, and strong winds and gales had overtaken them. By this time the wire that they were using (which was only a mooring wire), for towing was almost in shreds, and to make things more difficult another of the *Cheyenne's* propeller blades dropped off.

The *Chesapeake's* master, sensing a certain amount of danger, slipped the tow and stood off from the *Cheyenne* to await instructions from the company. Both ships had their engines running slowly to maintain steerage in the face of the storm.

In the latter part of February, when the company received the news about the *Cheyenne*, a telegram was sent to the *Iroquois* that was delivered on board by a tug. The orders stated that a tug would be coming alongside to give a supply of steam in order to be able to start preparing to put to sea and travel round to Falmouth for de-scaling of the hull. The ship would be fully manned twelve hours before she was due to sail. The tug duly came alongside and steam was put on board to get the auxiliaries started and water pumped into the boilers. Getting boilers started would have been a mammoth task without the aid of externally supplied steam, as the oil that was fed to the boiler had to be heated, and without steam the oil could not be heated or pumped. Steam was duly raised and the engine warmed through. The rest of the ship's company boarded and settled in and they set off for Falmouth

To the Chief Engineer's horror he found that none of the engineers had ever sailed with the *Iroquois* before; more to the point, some of them had never sailed in steamships before and had only been in motor ships. The Chief Engineer was so nervous about leaving the engine-room to such inexperienced hands that he stayed in the engine-room for the whole of the passage round to Falmouth.

The Thames estuary is well known for its fouling of ships' hulls, and although the *Iroquois'* hull was supposedly coated with anti-fouling paint, she was so encrusted with barnacles and marine growth that her speed was reduced by two knots. She dry-docked at Falmouth for descaling and minor repairs. The Chief Engineer was curious as to just how much marine growth there really was on the hull. The growth was scraped off into large wicker baskets before being hoisted by crane out of the dry dock. One of these baskets was weighed by the Chief Engineer, the number of baskets raised calculated, and hence the tonnage of fouling. This was calculated at eighty-five tons. With this amount of fouling preventing the smooth passage through the water, no wonder it slowed the ship down.

As soon as she was descaled and out of dry dock, the *Iroquois* was despatched at her best possible speed to meet the *Cheyenne* at an approximate position of lat.48° 52′ N, long.18° 56′ W on 9 March. The engineers must have pulled a few illegal strokes because the *Iroquois* clocked up a speed of 13.5 knots on her way to meet the *Cheyenne*, and this was faster than she had ever travelled. On 9 March the *Iroquois* was a hundred and fifty miles south of the *Cheyenne*, and the *Chesapeake* was dispatched to continue her voyage to Manchester.

Getting a line across to the *Cheyenne* this time was a different matter altogether. The *Iroquois* was unable to get very close to the *Cheyenne* because the seas were so high. A lifebelt was attached to a heaving line, and this was run out downwind for several hundred yards and after a lot of manoeuvring was eventually picked up by a crew member of the *Cheyenne* using a boat-hook.

On 11 March the *Iroquois* finally connected her towing hawsers to the *Cheyenne* at lat.49° 32′ long.17° 6′ W, and started the long tow home. By this time the weather had risen to what was known as a strong to moderate gale, and the *Iroquois* proceeded at reduced speed to save wear and tear on the towing gear. By 13 March both vessels were practically hove to because of the weather, but everything was holding well. The weather had abated by 16 March and the company radioed the *Iroquois* to advise the Master that it was up to his discretion whether to tow to Falmouth or London. The Master decided that as the weather was improving the *Iroquois* would tow the *Cheyenne* to her original destination of Thameshaven (London), and she docked there on 21 March, after being towed up the Thames by four tugs. She was back in service on 30 March.

The *Cheyenne* was torpedoed and attacked by gun-fire by U.53 and later sunk by a Royal Navy destroyer on 18 September 1939, to prevent her falling into enemy hands.

It is ironic to note that the *Chesapeake* left Eastham on the Manchester Canal on 26 April. The same year she was sailing through the Irish Sea, when she lost a propeller blade and had to return to port for repairs, and that the *Cheyenne* lost another propeller blade on 27 July the same year, while in passage from Aruba to Ellesmere, and yet another on 5 November the same year.

The *Iroquois*, it seems, was put back into semi-retirement as she was then laid up in the River Fal, Cornwall, on her return home in May 1932, until 17 December 1933 when she went into dry-dock for de-scaling. It is strange to note that although she was laid up in the River Fal, which is a quiet, narrow river, she was still not free from problems. On 23 December 1932 the Master of the *Iroquois* telephoned the London office of Anglo-American to say that during a heavy gale (force 10) that day the *Iroquois* had dragged her moorings and was close to St. Mawes Bank, if not touching it. The vessel at that time was drawing 20ft of water aft. Soundings had been taken and they also showed 20ft. The decision was taken to trim the forward cargo tanks by filling with water, thus lifting the stern. This was put into operation with success. She was remoored the next day and suffered no damage.

Several ships were moored together in the River Fal. The *Iroquois* was tied up to the *Invergordon*. One of the officers from one of these ships had his wife and family with him on board. His daughter, about twelve years of age and a non-swimmer, fell overboard between the two ships. The gap

*Above: Getting near to the* Cheyenne.
*Right: Just starting the tow.*

Chesapeake.

*Iroquois towing SS* Francunion *at Aruba in Dutch West Indies, 14 April 1934.*

*The* Francunion *in later years. (Courtesy of Esso.)*

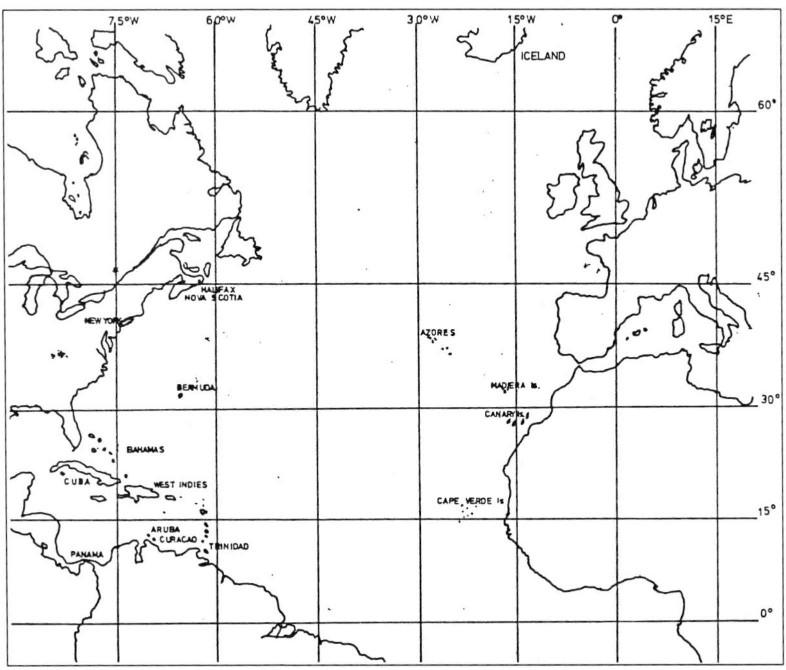


*The Atlantic Ocean.*

between was about three feet. When she surfaced she had the presence of mind to jam herself between the two vessels and continued to shout for help till she was lifted out.

March 1934 added mystery to the exploits of the *Iroquois*. At the beginning of March she took on a cargo at New Orleans and had discharged it at Thameshaven by 26 March, passing Dungeness on the 27th. Nothing was recorded on the voyage record cards till she passed Gibraltar on 3 May. This suggests something clandestine was taking place. Lloyd's List stated that the *Iroquois*, London, bound for Aruba, was in wireless contact with Fayal in the Azores on 2 April. There was no mention of her arriving at Aruba, but the photo is proof enough: it is dated 14 April 1934. Lloyd's List states that the *Iroquois* left Aruba—no date is given. The guess is that the *Iroquois* left Aruba in the Dutch West Indies with the *Francunion* in tow, possibly towing her as far as the Azores before continuing to Gibraltar. The *Francunion* arrived at Falmouth on 9 May. The *Francunion* had for years been coasting between Lake Maracaibo, Aruba, Trinidad and back to Maracaibo and Aruba until 1928. Prior to this she had been an oil depot ship stationed at Algiers and had moved to Aruba/Maracaibo in November and December 1924. During the 1930s there were some further ships placed under nominal British–Mexican ownership. One of these, the SS *Francunion*, was sent to the UK, and used for coasting and bunkering work, mainly in Southampton waters. She was later taken over by Anglo-American Oil Co in 1938, and transferred to Manchester and Liverpool, where she performed bunkering services during the war. She stayed there till 1949, when she was transferred back to Southampton. She was seen bunkering the *Queen Elizabeth* in 1954, and was scrapped in 1960. (The *Francunion* of 737 tons was built by Harland and Wolff, Govan, in 1921 and was at that time operated by Lago Shipping Co.)

In July 1934 Britain alone had over 3.5 million tons of shipping laid up.

Prior to 1934 the *Iroquois* would discharge her cargo at Thameshaven, and make the return trip to the US Gulf. In the years 1908–1914 the *Iroquois* and *Navahoe* were able to make an average of eight return trips to the US and turn-around time including loading of cargo could be achieved in two or three days. From 1919–1927 the turn-around time in the US had increased considerably, often taking several weeks, due to the congestion at the US ports. Remember that world demand for the liquid gold had increased enormously. After 1927 the turn-around time in the US had dropped to less than seven days, enabling the *Iroquois* and *Navahoe* to increase the number of voyages made from four in 1919 to seven in 1927. The 'Twins'' turn-around time at Thameshaven was usually completed in less than two days and this included their tank cleaning.

The *Iroquois* was designed to carry a mixed cargo by virtue of her many tanks and pumping arrangements. Occasionally, she would discharge a part cargo at Thameshaven and continue to other ports of call such as the Continental and Scandinavian ports. By 1934 the congestion in the US ports had eased considerably to the extent that she usually loaded mixed cargoes. By this time the size of the tankers had increased slightly, and only a few of Anglo-American's ocean tankers were able to travel up some of the inland waterways, and one of these was the *Iroquois*.

The *Iroquois* from then onwards often discharged a part cargo at Thameshaven, and would travel round the west coast of the UK to Barry Island and Avonmouth, on to Milford Haven and Liverpool and from there to Stanlow refinery on the Manchester Ship Canal. Her routing often took her to Glasgow. She continued on this sort of route, making six return trips a year and carrying out distribution, till she was called up for foreign service in World War II.

One of the more memorable feats carried out by the *Iroquois* was the towing out of submarine pipelines at Tripoli, Lebanon (at that time part of Syria) and also at Haifa, Israel (at that time Palestine) in June 1934. At that time there was a great deal of confusion in those ports, and up till then oil had to be transported to the coast by road tanker, pumped into tanker barges, transported out to the tankers and pumped on board.

Two pipelines twelve inches in diameter were then laid from the oilfields of Kirkuk, near Mosul, in northern Iraq all the way to Al Hadithah, where the pipeline split, one half passing through Syria and splitting up yet again to serve an oil terminal at Latikia and another at Tripoli. The other pipeline from Al Hadithah passed across western Iraq, over the river Euphrates, through Jordan and on to Haifa through the hills of Galilee to the Mediterranean Sea, a distance of 1,150 miles. Offshore oil terminals were then built at both Haifa and Tripoli, and this required submarine pipelines to be laid between the shore and the terminals. Each pipe weighed about a ton, and was towed out into the bay till a continuous pipe was formed between the shore and the terminals. This facility enabled tankers to be loaded out in the bays without having to enter port. The first stream of oil reached Haifa from Iraq on 15 October 1934. The *Iroquois* was ideally suited to this assignment and was used to tow the pipe-lines between the shore and the two terminals. (A sum of two hundred and ten thousand pounds from the British Government was granted towards the construction of the offshore terminals and reclamation of land at Haifa to facilitate the export of oil from the Iraq Petroleum Oil Company.) These oil-lines were replaced in 1952 by a single pipeline of thirty inches diameter to give greater capacity from Kirkuk to the Syrian terminal of Banias.

In 1934 the parent company Standard Oil decided to use its initials phonetically, and became ESSO.

In October 1934 major changes were made to the *Iroquois'* pumping arrangements, so that she could still conform to Lloyd's classification, and at the same time extra heating coils were added to her fuel oil lines.

On 21 June 1935 a German tanker, MV *D.L. Harper*, was fog-bound off the Lizard, Cornwall. The Master stopped the ship and dropped the anchor because he felt that the ship was in danger. A squall blew up and the ship dragged its anchor so much that she ran aground on rocks west of Lizard. Salvage tugs were sent out from Bristol and the six German-American passengers and crew of thirty-eight were taken off the ship by the local lifeboat the next day and taken to port. The tugs eventually managed to refloat the vessel on the 25th, after three unsuccessful attempts. There were however problems in towing her much further, as her pump-room was flooded with oil and water. Her engine-room was intact, although according to the *Iroquois'* 4th Engineer, Sydney Munsen, there was a lot of water about in the engine-room. She was then towed to Gyllyngvase Beach for safety sake. The *Iroquois* with her powerful pumps pumped out all her cargo of oil and bunkers, as well as the oil and water in the pumproom, and transported it to Hamburg. This enabled the three salvage tugs to start towing the *D.L. Harper* on 4 August to Hamburg without mishap. She arrived at Hamburg on 22 August but was not back in service till 29 November. This salvage of cargo resulted in the ship's company of the *Iroquois* receiving salvage money. The 3rd Engineer's share was five pounds. Quite a good bonus, as his salary was twelve pounds sixty-three pence a month.

Article from *The Times*, 27 June 1935:

> The R.N.L.I. has made awards amounting to twenty-seven pounds eleven shillings to the lifeboat crew and helpers at the Lizard, for the rescue of the crew of thirty-eight and five passengers from the *D.L. Harper* of Danzig, last Thursday when she was stranded in thick fog with heavy sea running.

(The *D.L. Harper* of 12,336 tons was built in 1933 and belonged to Standard Shipping Co of New York but was operated by Panama Transport Co.) She and her sister ships, all named after leading personalities in Standard Oil Co, were added to the Anglo-American Oil Co fleet that was operating in Panamanian waters. They were bought at discount prices as payment for oil supplied by Anglo-American Oil Co.

Contrary to claims that the *D.L. Harper* was bombed and sunk by German aircraft on 20 February 1942, she did survive the war, and quite often during World War II sailed in convoy with the *Iroquois*.

On 1 November the *Iroquois* had to put back to Belfast with engine trouble, when the engineers experienced trouble with the H.P. piston rod gland.

On leaving Haulbowline Dockyard, Cork Harbour on 7 November 1935, the *Iroquois* struck the dolphin at the entrance to the basin, damaging some of her plates. She then put into Belfast for repairs, which were extensive enough to keep her there till 12 November. No sooner had she left than loud noises were heard coming from the port engine H.P. cylinder. The port engine was stopped and it was found that the junk ring bolts had loosened and had found their way into the reduction pipe. She had to return to Belfast for repairs to her engines.

Some time in 1936 the *Iroquois* was fitted with a direction finder as an aid to navigation.

The *Iroquois* was grounded off Runcorn Dock in the Manchester Ship Canal on 24 October 1936. She managed to float off without assistance, but damaged one of her propellers.

On 11 August 1936 the 3rd Engineer, Leslie Birtles, was reported sick with difficulty in breathing and a fast heartbeat. He was kept off watch and told to rest on deck. Two days later he reported that he felt better and resumed watches. On arrival at Baton Rouge he was examined by the Standard Oil doctor who decided that he should rest for 3–7 days to reduce heart rate. He did not take the recommended rest, but was back at work with the 4th Engineer effecting repairs to the HP piston rod gland, a particularly hot and tiresome job. On the 15th, the 4th Engineer, Syd Munson, went to the 3rd Engineer's cabin and saw the 3rd Engineer in his bunk but did not disturb him. Four hours later the mess-room steward went to the same cabin and found that the 3rd Engineer had not moved. He then touched his arm and found it cold. He reported this to the Chief Engineer, Stan Hall, who summoned the Chief Steward and the Master, who pronounced him dead. He died of heart failure. By this time they were passing down the Mississippi River to New Orleans. When his body had been put ashore at New Orleans, the 4th Engineer, Syd Munson, was promoted to 3rd Engineer, but one thing he refused to do was to move into his 3rd Engineer's cabin.

The photo on the opposite page shows the *Iroquois* underway inwards up Eatham channel, tugs fast fore and aft, topmasts housed for safe passage under the bridges, *en route* to the Anglo-American terminal at Mode Wheel with a cargo of gas oil from Baton Rouge. The date was 24 August 1937 and was supplied by the 3rd Officer, at that time Martin Rutherford. The ship was being handled by Anglo's Manchester Ship Canal choice pilot, who in turn, was being hazed, harassed and insulted by the Captain, every time the ship touched the bank, which was frequently. Martin Rutherford states that the *Iroquois* handled badly in confined waters, she handled like 'a farm cart with a load of hay'.

In October 1937 the *Iroquois* departed from her normal scheduled transatlantic runs when she left Ellesmere Port on the Manchester Canal on the 6th with a cargo bound for Oxelosund in Sweden in the Baltic Sea. She was chartered for two return journeys to Gothenburg. A month later found her back on her run to Baton Rouge.

She reported grazing her bottom plates at Quarry Hole Point, Runcorn on 4 July 1938. No damage was sustained, and while outward bound, she grounded outside South Pass, New Orleans on 22 December 1938. She floated off without assistance.

*The* Iroquois *passing up Manchester Ship Canal, tugs fore and aft, with masts housed.*

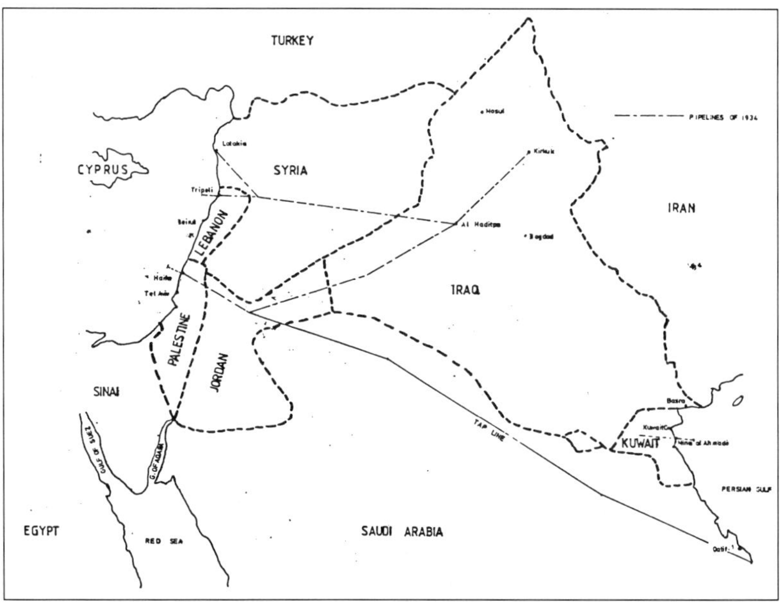


*The oil pipelines of the Middle East.*

*Above, left: The oil pipelines at Tripoli (Lebanon); right:* Iroquois, *in the background, doing her bit in 1934.*

D. L. Harper *aground on rocks at the Lizard.*

**SYRIAN WORKMEN** waterproofing a section of the miles of pipin that are being towed to sea from Tripoli. The pipes are to carr oil from the Irak wells direct to tankers.

*Article from the* Daily Express, *1 June 1934.*

# WAR SERVICE AGAIN

At the outbreak of World War II the *Iroquois* was the oldest vessel owned and operated by the Anglo-American Oil Co, the next oldest being the *Cadillac* of 12,074 tons, built in 1917 by Palmers of Newcastle.

From the outbreak of World War II to the end of 1942, the *Iroquois* made a total of thirty-two transatlantic crossings. For a tanker to manage this, without being damaged by the enemy, means that she must have been blessed with good fortune.

The first convoy that the *Iroquois* joined was KJ3, which was a fast convoy bound for the English Channel ports but without escort until some 200 miles south-west of Land's End. The Germans, acting on intelligence received, directed nine U-boats led by U37 to the attack, but by dawn on 14 October 1939 only three of them were on station. U45, commanded by Lieutenant Alexander Gelhar, was quickly on the attack, sinking three ships within the hour. This was the first attempt at a co-ordinated U-boat attack, a method which was to reap such dividends for the enemy in the years to come.

The KJ3 convoy escort's report was a bit scathing. In it he stated that the *Iroquois* was unable to steam without making continuous smoke. She was a danger to herself and to any convoy she was in. She was an oil-burner and either the firing installation needed attention or her engine-room personnel were incompetent. (Two other vessels were named as consistent smoke makers, though not in the same class as the *Iroquois*.)

The *Iroquois*, unlike many tankers of her time, never suffered any major fires on board. However in the afternoon of 26 March 1940, while in Govan Dry Dock, undergoing repairs, there was a terrific explosion. The tank top was blown up so far by the force of the explosion that it twisted part of the metal superstructure of the bridge. Two workmen were injured, and for the extent of the damage it was lucky that figure was so low. The *Iroquois* was in dry dock for her Lloyd's survey. Many men were working on the deck of the tanker when the cover of a larger bunker was blown high into the air. Several fire attachments boarded the vessel, and as they could not reach the fire owing to the fumes, the bunker was flooded with steam to quell the outbreak.

In September 1940 she entered dry dock again where she had a degaussing system fitted and was armed with a twelve-pounder gun, a 4.7″, a twin Hotchkiss on the poop deck and a single Hotchkiss above the bridge.

(Degaussing was a system preventing a ship having a magnetic field by passing a current through cables wrapped around the hull.)

The fitting of the twin Hotchkiss on the poop gave many a problem to the engineers. Each week target practice was carried out on the *Iroquois*. This involved dropping an oil drum over the side and towing it for some way while the gunners carried out their practice shoots. George Stokeld, the 2nd Engineer at the time, said that the vibration of the guns firing from the poop caused many of the light bulbs in the after section of the ship to either blow or fall out of their sockets. This was remedied thereafter by the bridge notifying the engine-room, and the engineers removing also all the light bulbs in the after section.

On 18 September the *Iroquois* ran aground on Lemans Bank off Hainsbro' Sands near Hull, while proceeding from London in convoy towards Methyl. She was able to be floated off some two hours later. When she had grounded she was drawing 20ft. 6ins., and when soundings were taken it was found that there was only 16ft. of water. The following day when she entered Largo Bay she was inspected by the Lloyd's surveyor and a seaworthiness certificate was issued. Again she was lucky! A year later at the same point about a dozen ships were wrongly led on to the Sands by an escort, six of them never getting off again. Many lives were lost on that terrible night, but even greater losses had been averted when the captains of the latter half of the convoy spotted the error in navigation and led the remainder of the convoy to safety.

On 11 November 1940 HX 86, a large convoy, started off at Halifax. It consisted of thirty-eight ships, which included the *Iroquois*, which had loaded kerosene at Aruba and was bound for Manchester. During this convoy the *Iroquois* was diverted to Belfast as her degaussing wires had burnt out, and this had rendered her compass useless. The convoy was escorted by HMS *Rodney* and AMC HMS *Voltaire* and the AMC HMS *Laconia* which was later torpedoed and sank with heavy loss of life in September 1942.

On 26 November the *Iroquois'* skipper, Captain James Jackson, died of coronary thrombosis, and the 1st Mate assumed command.

The *Iroquois* was at anchor off Alfred Dock, Birkenhead on 7 December 1940 when MV *Charles Racine*, having been fouled by the steamer *Almeda Star*, dragged her anchor and struck the *Iroquois* on her starboard bow. This collision holed the starboard after lifeboat and carried away the davits and their sockets. The sockets and davits were also damaged on the starboard lifeboat as well as a bit of damage to the superstructure.

(The *Almeda Star* was a 14,935-ton vessel that was used as a troop carrier, built in 1926 at Birkenhead, and owned by Blue Star Line.)

(The *Charles Racine* was a 9,957-ton motor vessel built by Odense Norway, and owned by Skibs A/S Snefonn.)

On 15 December, for the second time in her history at the same spot, whilst weighing anchor at the West Buoy moorings in the River Tyne, her port anchor fouled the moorings. On attempting to sight and clear anchor, the main driving wheel of the windlass broke, rendering the windlass useless.

During the night of 27 February 1941, while on convoy BHX 112, and during a heavy northerly gale, the *Iroquois* pooped a heavy sea carrying away the port lifeboat and davit. This gale continued with a falling glass and rising sea that necessitated the convoy heaving-to at 17.45 on the 28th at a position 61°.23′ N 12° 52′ W. The convoy was reformed as HX 112 and shaped course at 06.30 the next morning.

On 1 March, while in the same convoy, the *Iroquois* had to put back into Halifax, Nova Scotia, for engine repairs, which were completed on 8 March.

The *Iroquois* was principally built for the North Atlantic trade and it was envisaged that the cold would permeate throughout the whole of the vessel, to such an extent that heating pipes were installed on the bulkheads in both boiler and engine rooms. George Stokeld (2nd Engineer) felt that even in the middle of winter the engine-room was still hot and spent much of his spare time removing the pipes.

She consequently then joined convoy HX 115 which left Halifax on 17 March in company with about thirty other ships. When the convoy had reached a position of 150 miles south of Iceland, SS *Masunda* reported at 06.32 that the Master had seen a torpedo that had been fired from his port hand and by changing course had allowed the torpedo to pass. In taking this evasive action the torpedo had struck the *Germanic*. If the master of the *Germanic* had taken the same avoiding action the *Iroquois* would have been hit. MV *Bridgepool* opened fire at 06.42. The Master of the *Germanic* reported later that the torpedo struck the ship about ten feet below the water-line at the after end of the engine-room. After the deck officers and crew had abandoned ship and had cast off, they waited for fifteen minutes for the ship to go down. This was just as well as they saw someone flashing a light on the stricken vessel. They then returned to find the Chief and 2nd Engineer. They both had been knocked unconscious by the explosion. They were taken on board the lifeboats. At daylight they could see the *Hylton* (which had been torpedoed as well) in the distance, still afloat. By this time the decks of the *Germanic* were completely awash. The crews of *Hylton*, *Germanic* and *Limbourg* were rescued by the corvette HMS *Dianilla* and landed at Londonderry. The *Hylton* had been loaded with phosphates and blew up immediately the torpedoes had struck; in consequence there had only been two survivors. *California* gave the order to start making smoke to conceal the convoy at 06.48 and the signal was not rescinded till 08.00.

In the same action *Limbourg* had also been sunk by torpedo. The MV *Oakworth* minutes later sighted a submarine 100 feet off the port side of her and steaming on a parallel course on the surface. The guns on the *Oakworth* had been manned but owing to the position of the submarine had been unable to train on her. The *Oakworth* turned sharply with the intention of ramming the submarine, but the submarine increased speed very quickly and managed to get clear, but only by fifty feet. Subsequently HMS *Malaya II* dropped several patterns of depth charges after he established contact with the U-boat. The *Hylton*, *Germanic* and the *Limbourg* had been in the port columns. SS *Treverbyn* was on the starboard column. After the three ships had been torpedoed the *Treverbyn* spotted a U-boat on the surface travelling at high speed (about fifteen knots) with conning tower clearly visible at a range of 4,500 yds. The *Treverbyn* opened fire and the opening shot fell short, but the second hit the U-boat in the fore part of the conning tower and a dull red flame was seen. Thirteen shots were fired and the fifth also scored a hit on the after end of the sub. The U-boat stopped for a few minutes and then made off to the west of the convoy. The sub had first been observed prior to the attack on the convoy by HMS *Malaya II.* Several rounds had been fired by *Malaya II* before they lost sight of her. HMS *Malaya* and HMS *California* had been the ocean escorts for this convoy. *Hylton* and *Germanic* stayed afloat for a couple of hours with the decks awash and had to be sunk by HMS *Venomous* by a combination of depth charges and gunfire.

The U-boat that had attacked the convoy HX 115 had been U48 with Kapitan-Leutnant Herbert Schultze.

The positions of these ships in the convoy is shown overleaf.

(*Germanic* was a steamer of 5,352 tons built in 1936 at Hartlepool and operated by Sir Walter Cockerline.)
(*Hylton* was a motor vessel of 5,197 tons built in 1937 in Sunderland and owned by Hebburn Steamship Co.)
(*Masunda* was a steamer of 5,250 tons built in 1929 on the Clyde and operated by Maclay and McIntyre.)
(*Limbourg* was a Belgian motor vessel of 2,843 tons built at Hoboken and owned by CieNationale Belge de Trans Marine.)
(*Oakworth* was a motor vessel of 4,968 tons built in 1925 at Dumbarton and operated by Dalgliesh Steam Shipping Co.)
(*Bridgepool* was a tramp steamer of 4,845 tons built in 1924 at Hartlepool and owned by Pool Shipping Co.)

LAYOUT OF HX115 (SHOWING CARGOES CARRIED)

| | | | | | | | | |
|---|---|---|---|---|---|---|---|---|
| | | | | CALIFORNIA<br>COMMODORES FLAGSHIP | | | | |
| NORMAN PRINCE<br>SUGAR | HYLTON<br>WHEAT | BRITISH STATESMEN<br>BENZINE | NORWEGIAN<br>GENERAL | SAN CIRILO<br>GASOLINE | ARABIAN PRINCE<br>GENERAL | MALAYA II<br>GENERAL | COWRIE<br>FUEL OIL | BRITISH VALOUR<br>FUEL OIL |
| PRINCE WILLEM II<br>BAUXITE | GERMANIC<br>WHEAT | IROQUOIS<br>KEROSENE | EULIMA<br>GAS OIL | ATHELPRINCE<br>MOLASSES | CITY OF JOHANNESBURG<br>GENERAL | BOSTON CITY<br>GENERAL | TREFUSIS<br>GRAIN | TREVERBYN<br>STEEL LAMB |
| OAKWORTH<br>WHEAT LAMB | HERCULES<br>GENERAL | MASUNDA<br>WHEAT | PELEUS<br>WHEAT | ITTERSUM<br>GRAIN | GAND<br>STEEL SCRAP | BUESTEN<br>GASOLINE | NELLIE<br>GRAIN | ATHEL-DUCHESS<br>MOLASSES |
| | LIMBOURG<br>GENERAL | | | BRIDGEPOOL<br>STEEL LUMBER | | | | |

(*Treverbyn* was a steamer of 5,581 tons built in 1920 at Belfast and owned by Hains Shipping Co.)

On passing Belfast, which was a convoy dispersal point as well as a convoy mustering point, the remainder of the convoy was reformed off Mew Island and was on station by 01.00 on 5 April. The convoy was attacked by two enemy aircraft in lat.52° 12′ N long.05° 39′ W. The attacks were delivered separately but in quick succession. The first attack was made from the starboard bow, and the second from astern. Both were very low level attacks and both were concentrated on MV *Cape Verde* (a newly built vessel which had joined the convoy at Belfast) and were preceded by severe machine-gun fire. Three bombs were dropped from each plane in each attack, one bomb from the second aircraft scoring a hit on the *Cape Verde* in the vicinity of No. 5 hatch. Her damage was sufficiently bad to necessitate turning back and limping in to Belfast for repairs.

(The *Cape Verde* was a motor vessel of 6,914 tons built in 1941 at Glasgow and owned by The Good Hope Motorship Co.)

The next convoy that she joined, bound for the Clyde with a cargo of vaporising oil, was HX130 with ocean escorts HMS *Ramillies* and HMS *Derbyshire*. Experiments were made on certain vessels during this convoy with a preparation designed for either mixing with fuel oil or spraying over coal in order to reduce smoke, In the Convoy Commodore's report he noted that the smoke from those ships taking part in the experiment was noticeably less in comparison with other ships.

The following convoy, HX143, was a particularly large convoy containing seventy-three ships, and the *Iroquois* bound for the Clyde was carrying a cargo of gas oil.

At the end of September the *Iroquois* missed SC50 and fortunately joined SC51, a convoy consisting of thirty-seven vessels. SC50 lost one ship, the *King Malcolm* of 5,120 tons, when the convoy was attacked by U374. The *King Malcolm* had sunk in thirty seconds without any survivors. During convoy SC51 the steering gear of the *Iroquois* failed and she collided with the *Taxiarchis* and had to leave the convoy to carry out repairs. Three hours later she caught up with the convoy.

While in the River Mersey she was in collision with the same ship, and suffered damage to her bows. This collision was caused by her steering gear having jammed again.

(The *Taxiarchis* was a steamer of 4,221 tons built at Stockton in 1913, and operated by Theseus SS Co, Piraeus. Her name, translated from the Greek, means 'Master of the Rulers'.)

By this time 77% of all German-controlled shipping from Italy was sunk, mainly because of the forces operating from Malta. From the German point of view it was imperative that Malta was overrun, so that supplies could be ferried across the Mediterranean to North Africa. For the next few months something approaching 6,000 tons of bombs a month were dropped on Malta's airstrips, towns and villages. 'If the civilian population collapses, the whole fortress collapses,' wrote Sir William Jackson, Deputy Governor of Malta.

During the last three months of 1941 there was a lot of damage to vessels from the Atlantic storms. Gales of force 7 or more were recorded on fifty-three days and stragglers from convoys brought many more problems for escorts. Many ships arrived in port with heavy weather damage necessitating repair and subsequent delay. The weather, however, hampered the U-boat activities, and very few merchant ships were sunk in November and December. At this period many of the U-boats were being sent to the Mediterranean Sea.

On 12 December 1941 the United States of America joined in the war after Pearl Harbour was bombed.

During this part of World War II the *Iroquois* was used to carry kerosene to the UK. She loaded cargo at Aruba or Curacao and joined the convoy in the Bermuda section, joining the main convoy at Halifax, Nova Scotia, for her trip across the Atlantic. In most cases she discharged at either the Clyde ports or the Mersey ports.

The *Iroquois'* boilers were oil-fired but her galley, believe it or not, was coal-fired. This made her quite a rarity. At one time during World War II, the ship had ordered the usual twenty tons of coal for the trip, and someone in the Admiralty, thinking that this was a mistake, cancelled the order. Because of that the *Iroquois* missed the convoy. In early 1942 an oil-fired galley was installed.

The *Iroquois* left Liverpool at 12.30 on 22 February 1942 and proceeded as part of convoy ON102 for five days without incident until a position of 33°N 24°.30′ W was reached. The *Iroquois* then parted company with the convoy and sailed independently for Aruba in accordance with routeing instruction. A further five days without incident went by before they were advised by the Admiralty to alter their route in view of numerous submarine reports having been received from various vessels. Their course was altered in accordance with these instructions. Antigua in the West Indies was sighted and the *Iroquois* went through the Antiguan Passage about midnight on 15 March. At 3.15 on the next day the Master, a Captain Arthur Cook, was summoned to the bridge by the Third Officer who was on watch, who reported he had sighted what he thought to be a submarine about four or five miles ahead. The helm was put over to bring the enemy astern and the *Iroquois'* guns were trained on him. As soon as the sub saw the *Iroquois* change course he too put his helm over and gave them his silhouette to reduce the size of target. The *Iroquois* was about to send out a submarine attack message when he turned and it was only then noticed that it was an American patrol vessel. After identifying each other by flag signals and Aldis lamp they parted company.

At 17,00 the *Iroquois* sighted what was apparently a ship's lifeboat about six miles away. At this range only the sail could be seen and it was treated with suspicion until 17.40, when a second sail was sighted. Even then the bridge watch were suspicious, and it was not until a yellow flag was noticed that it was decided that they must be lifeboats. The sea was moderate, wind force 5, and excellent visibility. The *Iroquois* was making ten and a half knots on a course 247 degrees but zig-zagging all the time, as it was known that there was a submarine in the vicinity.

The course of the *Iroquois* was altered in the direction of the lifeboats but still zig-zagging, and she steamed within twenty feet of the first lifeboat (a motor boat under sail) when he started his motor and came alongside. The survivors came aboard and the lifeboat was cast adrift. The *Iroquois* then went to the assistance of the second lifeboat which by now was about three miles distant, and rescued the survivors from this boat. The rescue operation was carried out at 19.00 on 16 March in a position 14°N 66°W. Twenty-seven survivors were picked up from the first lifeboat and twenty-one from the second. Some of the survivors were covered in oil, and two of them were suffering from burns.

The survivors were from the Panamanian tanker *Penelope*. She had been carrying a cargo of light crude oil from Caripito to Halifax and had been struck by three torpedoes and had sunk about thirty-five miles from the pick-up position. The submarine was a French one but had been manned by Germans.

At daybreak on the 17th the *Iroquois* received a wireless message from the *Acacia* stating that she was being shelled and machine-gunned by a submarine and was about thirty miles from the *Iroquois*. Captain Cook did not break radio silence for fear of giving away his position. With nearly a hundred people on board he felt it imperative to reach the safety of port as soon as possible. The survivors were landed and taken to hospital when the *Iroquois* docked at Aruba. One of the survivors, a seventeen-year-old, died on board the *Iroquois* as a result of his burns, and was buried at sea that day. Captain Cook received a commendation for the action he had taken. He had been torpedoed twice. The first time was on the twelfth day of war while he was serving on the *Cheyenne* when she had been unarmed. Before the war the *Penelope* had traded from Aruba and the west coast ports to Europe and the Mediterranean ports, and during the war between Aruba and Guiria.

(The MV *Penelope* was a 8,436-ton twin-screwed tanker built in Germany in 1925, and belonged to the Panama Transport Co.)

The *Iroquois* joined SC78 loaded with tractor oil for the Clyde in company with eighteen other ships in fair weather on 5 April 1942. The convoy could not be formed up till late in the evening due to the *Iroquois* and one other ship still being at anchor with motor-boats alongside at the time of sailing. At 22.50 that evening dense fog was encountered which lasted for thirty-six hours. The convoy met a NNW gale on the 9th which started very suddenly accompanied by low visibility. Three ships dropped out of the convoy and returned to Halifax.

(The Convoy Commodore's report was a little tardy and stated: The *Iroquois* is a very old tanker and is unhandy, both as regards steering and variations in speed. It is not clear how much of her erratic behaviour was due to the ship herself or to her handling which was on occasions definitely at fault. On several occasions she was a danger to other ships in the convoy and she was unsuitable as a column leader. It is only fair to state, however, that during thirty-six hours of dense fog, her leadership was very satisfactory.)

A Malta-bound convoy was sent from Glasgow with essential supplies in June 1942. The whole convoy was decimated. One of the ships in this convoy was the *Kentucky*, a 9,308-ton tanker built in 1942 for Texas Oil Co and operated by Anglo-American Oil Co. She was bombed and sunk in the Mediterranean while on Admiralty Charter.

On 11 July, while in convoy ONS102, the *Iroquois* had to put back to Bermuda for repairs to her starboard fan engine and was not able to leave till the 16th. She sailed to Curacao where it was discovered that she had leakages in her tanks; this meant a stay in dry dock and she finally left there after repairs on 7 September. Before she moved into dry dock she bumped into MV *Herbruna* causing slight damage to the break of the forecastle head of the latter vessel. There was an easterly force 4 wind blowing at the time.

While the *Iroquois* was berthing at the Asiatic Wharf in New York on 5 October, she made contact with the stern of MV *Strinda* who was berthed alongside. There was a strong ebb tide running. The collision caused damage to the *Iroquois* amounting to eight starboard fore-deck stanchions bent and one foremast stay parted, but there was no damage to the *Strinda*. There were, however, two iron bollards carried away from the jetty which had been holding the after moorings. (The MV *Strinda* was a Norwegian 10,973-ton tanker built in Germany in 1937 and owned by A/S Ludwig, Mowinckel Rederi.)

George Stokeld, 2nd Engineer 1942–45, said that the arrangements that fed the toilet cisterns were not so good, as the sanitary pump often packed up. On one occasion after coming off watch at 08.00 he went to the toilet and when he had finished he pulled the chain. Nothing happened, no flushing took place. When George looked down into the toilet pan there was an enormous rat sitting there, looking up at him. He comment was: 'What would I have told the missus if it had bitten my private parts?'

On 18 July 1942 the Eagle Oil Transport tanker SS *San Gaspar* was torpedoed near Tobago, with a loss of ten crew and two gunners, at a position lat.10° 30′ N, long.60° 27′ W, by the German U-boat U-575, and was badly damaged by fire, so badly that the Master, Captain D.K. Blyth, was forced to abandon her although she was still floating. The U-boat surfaced shortly afterwards, interrogated Chief Engineer J.M. Sayer's lifeboat and presented the survivors with a bottle of cognac. Despite the damage to her she was towed on the 23rd by tugs to Trinidad, where the remainder of her cargo was discharged. The surveyor's report on 14 October stated that the *San Gaspar's* bridge and engineers' accommodation were absolutely gutted and that Nos. 6, 7 and 8 tanks on the starboard side were badly holed and her forward pumproom was flooded. The *San Gaspar* was roughly patched up and pumped dry. The *Iroquois* started towing her on 19 December, bound for New York, but was diverted to Key West, in the Straits of Florida, for further patching up to be carried out. The estimate for repairs was put at $162,160 with an estimated time of two hundred hours for the repairs to be carried out. She arrived there with the *San Gaspar* on 29 December. The *San Gaspar* was back in service on 6 January 1943, and survived the war, and was often in convoy with the *Iroquois*. The *San Gaspar* had amongst her cargo 3,000 drums of aviation spirit and 17,000 drums of fuel oil, as well as cased goods.

(The *San Gaspar*, 12,910 tons, was a tanker built in 1921 at Newcastle and operated by The Eagle Oil Co. She was scrapped in 1954.)

By August 1942 Malta was desperately short of fuel oil and other essential supplies, and it was decided by the Admiralty to mount 'Operation Pedestal'. This called for a fast convoy of sixteen knots and therefore the *Iroquois* was spared, this time! Only two freighters and the SS *Ohio* made it to Malta. The *Ohio* only made it because she was lashed to two other naval vessels which virtually held her afloat. The *Ohio*, with decks literally awash, was carried into Grand Harbour. A scene of mass hysteria reigned as the Maltese thronged to the harbour-side, cheering themselves hoarse and weeping with joy, cheering the gallant ship. Fifteen vessels had started out on the convoy to Glasgow, and during the journey they had been subjected to aerial bombardment as well as attack by both submarine and surface vessels.

(The *Ohio* was a fast tanker of 9,265 tons built in 1940 in Pennsylvania and operated by Texas Oil Co.)

On 18 August 1942 Portugal gave the Allies two bases in the Azores. The island bases of Fayal and Tereica were given in exchange for arms and guaranteed protection against German attacks. Having these bases in the Azores meant that Allied shipping could be protected by forces operating from these bases, and thus that the theatre of war attention could now be transferred from the Atlantic to the Pacific Ocean.

The Allied landings in north-west Africa on 8 November marked the turning point in World War II, as well as the victory at El Alamein.

1 December 1942 saw the *Iroquois* with more engine trouble and she had to put back into Guantamano Bay. These repairs took eight days and she left for Trinidad on the 9th.

By late 1942 the *Iroquois*, in common with many other tankers, had been fitted with a spar deck, which was a mass of girders that were welded to the deck, so that in addition to carrying oil cargo from the US and Aruba, she carried planes and other equipment from Canada and the US to the UK, and like most ships during the war, was often grossly overloaded.

Allied shipping losses in the first quarter of 1943 were disastrous: January 203,000 tons, February 359,000 tons and March 627,000 tons. In fact, two convoys from Halifax alone lost 141,000 tons for the price of one U-boat sunk.

March 1943 found the *Iroquois* leaving Avonmouth with Captain Collister as Master. On arrival in New York it was found that the Master was suffering from diabetes and had to be put ashore. The Chief Officer, Jack Palmer-Felgate, was promoted to Master.

Total Axis surrender in North Africa in May 1943 meant that the Mediterranean route to Allied shipping was now open. This gave a bonus of two million tons carrying capacity, since the Suez Canal was available for use once more. Because of the increased safety in this area, ships of a slower speed could now be used on convoy.

On 29 May 1943 the Allies planned to launch an offensive against the Caroline and Marshall Islands in the south-west Pacific. This plan was approved by the Combined Chiefs of Staff. These islands had for some time been held by the Japanese.

On 6 September 1943 the *Iroquois* was requisitioned OHMS and sailed from New York with a cargo of aviation spirit for Malta and fuel oil for Bizerta, arriving at Malta safely on 26 October. Believe it or not, she had been scheduled to sail on a homeward-bound convoy from New York, but her windlass broke down on weighing anchor and she missed her planned convoy. Most of her cargo of fuel oil was used to fuel the fleet at Bizerta and the aviation spirit was discharged at Malta. The remainder of her fuel oil was used to refuel various naval ships that came alongside and took what they termed a 'spoonful at a time' so that the crew thought it would be a long monotonous time before they got rid of the rest of the load. Fortunately in the end the remainder was transferred to another tanker. At that time the famous tanker SS *Ohio* could be seen lying against the breakwater. This took several weeks, and she left Malta on 15 November, arriving back at New York on 20 December.

On one of these trips one of the engine-room greasers tried to attack the ship's carpenter with an axe, having kicked in his cabin door. The carpenter, in panic, had grabbed the first thing that had come to hand, which happened to be a knife, and lunged at the greaser. The knife penetrated the greaser's stomach, slicing it open, and he later died as a result of his wounds.The greaser was considered a no-good Scotsman, who when in drink was a vicious bully, and had beaten up most of the engine-room crew (but not officers) who happened to cross him at the wrong time. 'Chippy' was considered a great man, quiet, and very popular with everybody on board. 'Chippy' was put in prison on arrival in New York until the coroner's court hearing, where he was completely cleared and released. For his own good he was transferred to another vessel, as the greaser had had a few Scots friends left on the *Iroquois*.

For the next six months she plied across the Atlantic several times between New York and the Moroccan port of Casablanca and the Mediterranean ports of Gibraltar, Oran in Algeria, and Bizerta in Tunisia. Oran had for some time been one of the operating ports for 'Operation Torch' for the invasion of Italy. One this voyage the *Iroquois'* spar deck was used for the transportation for landing craft. She was seen transferring oil to the tanker *Empire Garden* in Horta harbour, Fayal Island, in the Azores on 28 March. The *Empire Garden*, of 8,923 tons, had been built in Germany as the *Gedania* in 1919 and as such had been converted to carry fuel and supplies to German commerce raiders and U-boats operating in the Atlantic. She was also used to bring prisoners taken from sunken ships back

Iroquois *towing floating workshop with tug aft on left-hand side followed by floating dry dock, and astern of this on right-hand side large war supply barge.*

to Germany. She was captured near Iceland on 4 June 1941 by HMS *Marsdale*, renamed, and put into British service at Glasgow on 30 July 1941, operated by the Ministry of War Transport.

26 December 1943 found the *Iroquois* entering dry dock for an extensive refit for the next stage in her history.

By 31 January 1944 there were Allied landings in the Marshall Islands, and on 17 February Eniwetok was captured by the Allies, and by the end of February there were also Allied landings in the Admiralty Islands (north-east of New Guinea). 40,000 troops took part in these assaults.

On the evening of 1 February about forty bombers attacked UGS30 (of which the *Iroquois* was part) off Oran. The long-range fighters broke up the enemy formation. One ship was sunk and one damaged.

By March 1944 the Battle of the Atlantic was virtually over, as the U-boat packs had suffered heavy losses. Because of this, the Atlantic Ocean at least was a safer place.

On 26 June 1944 the *Iroquois* was drafted on to what could be loosely called special assignments, and it is interesting to recall the experience of Donald MacArthur who was an AB at the time. It is suspected that the

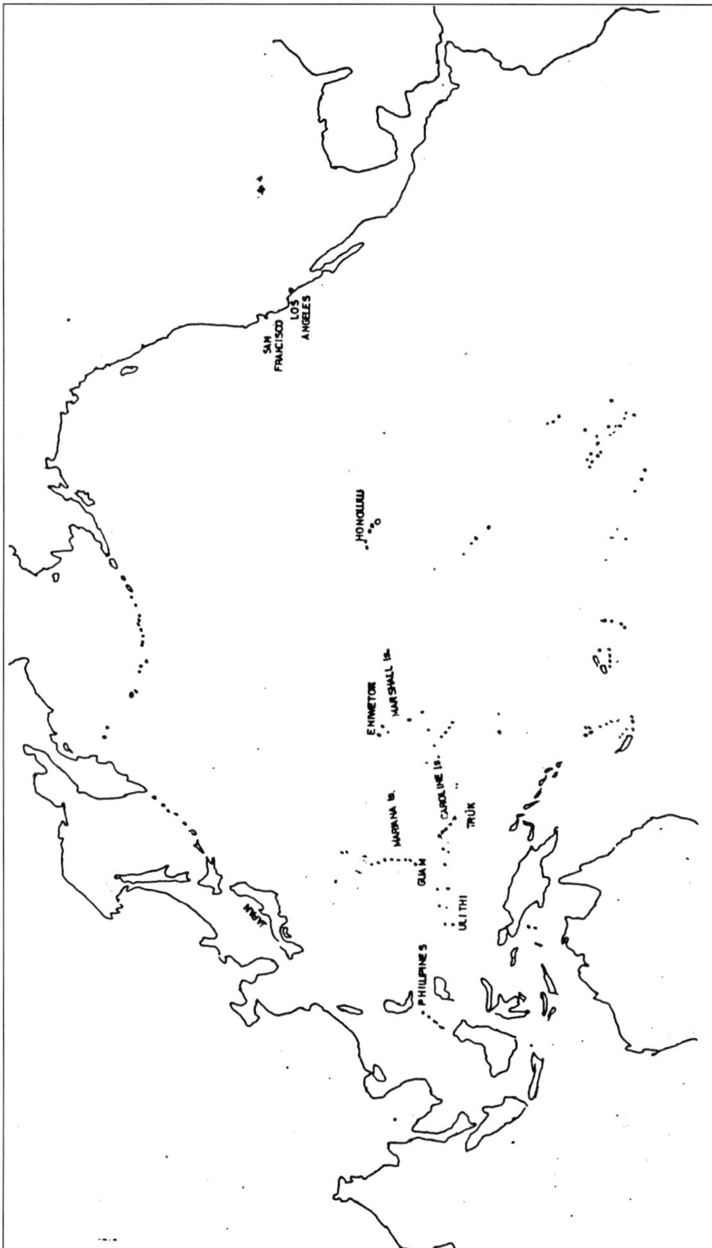


*The Pacific Ocean.*

American end of Anglo-American started 'pulling strings' for the benefit of the Americans. She left New York, sailed down to Guantanamo Bay (SE Cuba) and on to Caripito (Venezuela), eastwards to Trinidad in the West Indies and back to Aruba (Dutch West Indies). From there on 17 July she journeyed on to Cristobal on the eastern side of the Panama Canal. One day later she was through and arrived at Balboa on the Pacific side of the canal on 26 July, something she had only done once before, in 1922. The long haul then started north-westwards to Pearl Harbour, unescorted, and she arrived there on 24 August. However this was not without incident. The Chief Cook scalded himself badly whilst cooking fish in a deep pan of boiling fat. The ship had rolled and his arms went into the fat. After some days a US plane flew over the *Iroquois*, communications were made by Aldis lamp, and the *Iroquois* was directed to the nearest US base which was Johnston Island, where the cook was put into hospital. He was picked up by the *Iroquois*, quite recovered, some six months later. On this trip she had travelled a distance of about 3,000 miles.

A short trip (from then onwards she was always escorted by the American fleet) across to San Francisco for dry-docking (she had not been in dry dock for over two years) and she then loaded and went back to Pearl Harbour, arriving there on 2 October. It was decided to make full use of the *Iroquois'* potential by re-introducing her to towing, in addition to her oil- and deck-cargo-carrying capacity. Four days rest before she left for the Marshall Islands in Micronesia. While leaving Pearl Harbour with pilot on board, during the operation of connecting up tow, the *Iroquois'* quarter came into violent contact with the towed ship's overhang on bow; a lifeboat davit was damaged and made unusable. The American Fifth Fleet had its own service force of tankers, tenders and floating dry dock, but the *Iroquois* also acted as a support vessel for the US Navy by transporting oil between bases, where the cargo was off-loaded there into American Naval tankers, rather than replenishing individual ships as they came along. Every item of war supply had to be transported to the scene of the action.

This group of widely separated atolls had been captured by the Japanese from the Germans in World War I, and had been mandated to the Japanese in 1920, together with the Caroline Islands.This mandate prohibited the building of any military bases on the islands, but reconnaissance planes and submarines had revealed fortifications on several of the islands, including Eniwetok. By the time these islands were recaptured not a single Japanese aircraft was serviceable. Seven hundred aircraft were used in this assault.

The Americans badly needed a naval base before the Japanese mainland could be attacked. The choice fell on Ulithi, and it was seized on 23

September 1944. The taking of Ulithi meant that the United States had splendid naval and air bases within easy striking distance of the Philippines. Ulithi Atoll had a superb natural harbour and quickly became the main advanced base of the Third Fleet.

In Pearl Harbour the *Iroquois* joined up with other towing vessels to form a convoy of vessels which was predominantly under the American flag, and which was to travel at a speed of only five knots. This convoy arrived in Eniwetok in the Marshall Islands (long.163°E lat.12°N), a distance of 2,300 miles, on 22 October for an eight day stopover. During this time while the convoy was at anchor a Japanese submarine torpedoed and sank another tanker. They then travelled on to Ulithi, a tiny island in the Caroline group of islands (long.140°E lat. 10°N), a further 1,000 miles. The *Iroquois* journeyed around the Micronesian Islands, back and forth through Kossol Passage in the Palau Islands, and finally left the Islands on 11 December.

She was back in Pearl Harbour on 18 December before going on to San Pedro where she again loaded (one of the few occasions she was in port for Christmas) and left after four weeks, arriving at San Francisco on 29 January. She put into Pearl Harbour with a tow on 23 February and back to San Francisco (for dry-docking and loading) and San Pedro, leaving there on 30 May for a trip back to Pearl Harbour, where she arrived on 13 June.

On one of these towing missions to the Micronesian Islands the tow was more than a mile long and consisted of three vessels: a floating dry dock with a tug inside; a large barge; and astern of that a smaller barge loaded with ammunition. A still greater feat was when she towed a floating workshop, a huge lighter and a tug that was lashed to its side.

While the *Iroquois* was at anchor with several other American vessels at Ulithi Atoll, a Japanese (Kamikaze) suicide submarine was spotted. Fortunately it was captured before it could attach itself to any of the vessels.

The days on these passages were often long and monotonous, steaming along at such a slow speed, then often spending several days at anchor among the islands. The refrigerators and storerooms were usually pretty empty by the time they returned to the American ports, where they were re-provisioned, and repairs were authorized. Dehydrated potatoes, vegetables and eggs were not that appetizing. The flour and consequently the bread was hardly ever free from weevils, which was common to most ships.

Donald MacArthur states that he enjoyed a good comradeship on board the *Iroquois* but occasionally this was spoilt when they had to replenish crew from Ellis Island. (Ellis Island, New York, was where deserters from ships were kept and then used to replenish ships that were under-manned. Most of them were undesirables.)

Another story related by Donald MacArthur was that each time the *Iroquois* reached a US port the Captain always made arrangements for them all to give blood 'in the interest of the war effort.' They were very happy with this arrangement and they considered it rather generous, as it meant more shore leave. It was some twenty years later, when Donald MacArthur was piloting a ship in Milford Haven whose Captain had been the Chief Officer of the *Iroquois* during the war, that he enlightened Donald MacArthur that all the time they were giving blood the Captain of the *Iroquois* had been collecting and pocketing the dollars. Blood money!!

The story told about the *Iroquois* towing a floating dry dock from Bermuda to Pearl Harbour, that was so large that one side of it had to be flooded, and that it was towed sideways through the Panama Canal, is just not true, although there are several references to it.

## THOSE CONVOYS

The *Iroquois* usually loaded her cargo at Aruba, or on one or two occasions at Baytown or Curacao. From there she usually sailed independently to Bermuda, which was an ocean convoy assembly point. In the early part of the war convoys moved from Bermuda to New York and from there to the UK. By 1940 New York was becoming so congested that convoys were routed from Bermuda to Halifax (Nova Scotia), which then became the main assembly point. The convoys from Halifax were prefixed by the letters HX followed by the convoy number. The sections from Bermuda were prefixed BHX. The convoys usually left Halifax at four-day intervals. The convoys from Halifax that were able to travel in excess of ten and a half knots were considered fast and were prefixed HXF. Normally the *Iroquois* was scheduled to join HX convoys but on several occasions missed the HX convoy and joined a slow convoy prefixed SC, which usually travelled at a speed of eight and a half knots. These slow convoys tended to have a greater number of escorts. On leaving the UK the main convoy assembly points were the outer reaches of the Clyde and the Mersey. These convoys were prefixed OB, ON or ONS (slow convoy). The fact that the *Iroquois* missed a certain convoy was often to her advantage, as the scheduled convoy was sometimes attacked. There is a surprising lack of records regarding lists of outward-bound convoys. In the Admiralty convoy reports some ships (especially the Greek ones) were severely criticized for their poor station-keeping and their making excessive smoke. Some ships were complimented on the quality of their station-keeping and signals. However the *Iroquois* rarely got a mention either way.

# LATER MISSIONS AFTER THE WAR

By this time the war in Europe had come to an end (8 May 1945) and it was felt that the *Iroquois* could perform useful services nearer home. On 3 July she started her long journey back, arriving at the western approaches to the Panama Canal. She put into Curacao (part of the Dutch West Indies [Antilles]) on 9 July, picking up a cargo of oil before making her way across to Purfleet without the ship being subject to blackout (what a change), arriving on 24 July. Mrs Palmer-Felgate, who had said goodbye to her husband in March 1943, journeyed down to the Purfleet in August with the wife of one of the radio officers, to meet up with their husbands. As the taxi took them down the road to the *Iroquois'* berth they passed two officers by the side of the road. 'Isn't that your husband?' said one of them to the other. 'So it is, I didn't recognize him!' said the other.

Shortly after this discharge of cargo, the Far East war ended, and for several weeks the *Iroquois* lay in the Thames, upstream from Gravesend (near Erith). In the early stages the anchorage was poor and the ship dragged anchor nearly every tide, until eventually arrangements were made to moor the ship to a mooring buoy, using the starboard anchor cable. This was successful.

On 24 August a cargo of creosote pitch was loaded at Thameshaven for Saltend (Hull), after which the tanks were cleaned prior to arrival for dry-docking at the Tyne on 3 September. What a cargo to put in a ship before dry-docking!

On 14 September 1945 the *Iroquois* left the UK after having dry-docked at Middle Dock, Shields, and sailed for Haifa (Israel), which at that time was part of Palestine, arriving there on 27 September. On moving berth in Haifa, with the pilot on board, she was weighing anchor when a nut came adrift on the pistol of the forward cylinder cover. This in turn rendered the windlass inoperable, so it was impossible to raise the remainder of cable and anchor. The Pilot and Master decided to drag anchor and twenty-three fathoms of cable remaining into shallower water under the vessel's own power. The port cable was slipped at second shackle and was buoyed. When cargo loading operations and repairs to the windlass had been completed on 6 October the cable and anchor were recovered. On another occasion, 22 November, while in the Petroleum Basin, Haifa, she bumped the jetty with her starboard bow while coming alongside, causing damage to her shell plating in the fore deep tank, and while at the Shell Co buoys, Port Said, Egypt on 27 November she was turning seaward when she grounded lightly on the banks of Shell Co installations. Tug *Agile* was assisting at the time. (The *Agile* was a steam tug built in 1924 at Marseilles, France and operated by Canal Maritime de Suez.)

On 1 January 1946, the *Iroquois* came off Government service. On 15 February she experienced heavy weather conditions with winds force 7 and very rough seas with heavy swell. The speed of the vessel was reduced as she was labouring and shipping heavy seas fore and aft. For the next five months she was refuelling, at Alexandria, the troopships and naval craft transiting the Suez Canal, returning from the Far East after the cease of hostilities. (Alexandria was still one of the major naval bases in the Mediterranean.) In addition to the fuel oil carried from Haifa to Port Said she used to carry a part cargo of paraffin wax (for candles, etc.) This was in the form of 18″ cube bales, and was loaded into the dry hold (forward) and discharged with the ship's winches and derricks into a barge alongside. One of the refuelling exercises took her to Piraeus which was quite a break away from the 'shuttle' runs, but not without a bit of adventure. Before leaving Haifa on this occasion the Master was advised by the Haifa Naval Control (RN) that the depths in the approach channel to Port Piraeus were uncertain, as the *Iroquois* was the first large ship to enter since the end of the war in Europe. So upon arrival off the port of Piraeus she anchored while the 2nd Officer, Joe Burrowdale, was sent off in a motor lifeboat to make a survey of the channel using a hand lead-line and a notebook. It must have been successful, because the *Iroquois* berthed the next day without touching bottom. She continued refuelling until 7 March 1946 when she discharged her cargo and dry-docked at Alexandria, where it was found that she had some fractured plates in way of No. 6 tank.

In 1946 the Kuwait Oil Co, having produced crude oil, needed to export it, but had no suitable port. It was decided to use a sealine berth at Fuhayhil on the Persian Gulf coast, using submarine pipelines. The *Iroquois*, having been trading in the eastern Mediterranean, was chartered to tow these pipelines from the shore out to sea. Each pipeline was 10″ in diameter and approximately a mile long. The Deck Officers on board *Iroquois* had never heard of Fuhayhil, in fact the Admiralty Pilot book described it as a fishing village, and it appeared on the largest scale chart as a few dots. Nevertheless they found it.

She then passed through the Suez Canal journeying on to Fuhayhil (Iran) arriving there on 8 April. It was planned to arrive at Fuhayhil after noon, Monday, hoping the Chief Officer could produce a good astral position at dawn, and this would be followed up with a solar position at noon. Unfortunately the sky was overcast therefore no fixed position, only dead reckoning. The 2nd Officer managed to get one 'snap' of the sun mid-morning which was far from being a dependable fix, so the Master had to decide when and where to alter course and head due west in towards the shore, bearing in mind the proximity of several low-lying unmarked islands. He made a good decision as it turned out, but they had to proceed very slowly, sounding their way in with a hand lead-line. (In those days there were no echo-sounders, gyro-repeaters or radar, and in that area no lighthouses or buoys.) As the sun swung towards the west, they could see no more than two or three miles through the haze. Fortunately the shore gang, headed by two Master Mariners, saw them approaching from the east, and realizing their plight, set off to meet them in a large motor boat. This was the first thing that they in the *Iroquois* actually saw, and they thought it was an arab dhow. Captain Moore (from BP) supplied them with some hand-made charts, so they were able to anchor safely about a mile offshore.

Apart from three black oil tanks on the rise of the desert, two pipelines and their miniature railways lying up the slope, a few tents and the signal gantry, there was nothing on the beach. The direction in which they had to tow was marked by a few forty-gallon oil drums moored to concrete blocks, forming a straight line from the beach.

The *Iroquois* was manoeuvred into position, with two anchors down, stern to the beach, about half a mile off. Two BP tugs from Abadan were used to hold her against the wind and current until the tow started.

The Master, assisted by one of the shore captains, was on the bridge. The 1st Officer looked after the anchors and the two tugs. The 2nd Officer and his gang were in charge of the towing winch and the handling of the 7″ circumference steel wire. There was a ship's engineer in attendance in the towing winch house.

## THE TOW

The first consideration was to send the end of the wire ashore. The eye of the wire consisted of a steel thimble and splice, together about seven feet long and too heavy for men to handle so it had to floated ashore to avoid underwater obstructions. It was made fast to an old dhow. This in turn was towed ashore by Caterpillar tractors chugging up the desert. Once the eye was ashore, it was shackled to the sea-sled. This was a box-like

*Ploughing through the heavy weather of Alexandria, 1945.*

*Main deck in heavy weather. Note sea on main deck; trunk deck is dry.*

Iroquois *at Haifa breakwater, painted out in wartime colours, 1945.*

*Above: In Alexandria dry dock, 1945. Note detachable blades.*
*Left: Pipeline and the miniature railway, Kuwait.*

Iroquois *at anchor after towing first pipeline (see shadow under water). Second pipeline being prepared for following day.*

*Seaward end of pipeline attached to sea-sled.*

construction, bolted on to and supporting the seaward end of the pipeline, to keep the pipeline clear of the sea bottom and any obstructions during the tow. It looked rather like an old fashioned railway snow-plough.

The railway resembled a miniature railway and supported four-wheeled 'dollies', which in turn supported one mile of 10″ pipeline, which was coated with a bitumastic covering. As the pipeline moved forward, the dollies fell off the end of the line into a 'dolly-pit', to prevent obstruction. Each dolly was manned by an Arab workman carrying a flag. In the event of any problem with the dolly, the Arab would raise his flag and scream his head off . . . Nothing happened.

To oversee the whole of the shore-side operation a platform was erected that also acted as a signal gantry. It was rigged with three red signal flags, this being the only means of communication once the tow had started. (The use of an Aldis lamp would have been too slow.) The signals were as follows:

| | |
|---|---|
| 1st Flag: | Start heaving on the wire. (To 1,100 feet, then brakes on drum.) |
| 2nd Flag: | Proceed slow ahead. |
| 3rd Flag: | Tow at full power. |
| 1st Flag down: | Power eased off, but continue towing. |
| 2nd Flag down: | Stand by to stop. All except one brake taken off drum. |
| 3rd Flag down: | Stop. (Stop really did mean stop, because only about 15–20 feet of pipeline remained on dry land.) |

While the tow was underway, the wire was bar tight, so an immediate release of the brakes caused the wire to scream like a thread off a bobbin, as the load came off the tow. Once the tow had started and the pipeline was moving, both of the *Iroquois'* anchors were weighed, but were kept in a state of readiness to let go again after the operation was complete. Once the brakes had been released the vessel was of course almost stopped in the water, so she was anchored and allowed to settle to her anchor, but during this period a careful watch had to be kept on the wire so that no weight came on it that was sufficient to disturb the end of the pipeline.

Eventually, when everything had settled down, divers went to disconnect the shackle from the pipeline wire. However, they were very quickly pulled back to the surface as they had found a large number of sharks in the vicinity. The wire was eventually unshackled and hove in on to the drum, washing and scrubbing away the mud in the process. The wire was inspected for any sign of damage, and the winch was carefully checked over by the engineers. The following day the same exercise was repeated successfully but with the same problem with the sharks.

It will be noticed that upon the first signal from the shore (1 flag) the wire had to be hove in to 1,100 feet. Naturally, before this was attained, it was expected that the pipeline would have started to roll down the railway. On the first day this did not happen, and they discovered that the *Iroquois* had moved stern first on to the beach in spite of the two anchors being down to hold her head. Naturally, it had all happened very slowly and gently, so no damage had been done, but the whole exercise had to be restarted after the *Iroquois* had been re-positioned, only this time the engines were used Dead Slow Ahead, together with the weighing of the anchors, and the wire was heaved in to 1,100 feet.

The *Iroquois* spent four days towing the 10″ diameter pipes out to the offshore terminal. A new pipeline had been laid from the Kuwaiti oilfields and down to Fuhayhil. The offshore oil terminals this time were a distance of four miles offshore. At that time the Kuwait Government was anxious to get into exporting oil, and an offshore installation was an easier proposition than shore-based terminals.

Construction of the South Pier was then started, with berths 1, 2, 3, 4, 5 and 6 for tankers; berths 7 and 8 were built as tug berths and fuelling points. Berths 9 and 10 were added on completion, and at first were used for discharge of dry cargo, but oil lines were later extended to these berths as well.

In the late 1950s, sea berths C, D and J were laid by Wimpey Barge, assisted by the Jetty Maintenance Department and Marine Department.

The North Pier, berths 11, 12, 15 and 16 were commissioned in 1962, and the Sea-Island Berth was constructed eight miles offshore to the east, and was commissioned in 1966. These terminals were the ones responsible for the giant oil slick that was released during the Kuwait–Iraq war of 1990–1991.

## THE WINDLASS

The cable-lifting machine and rope drums were situated on the forecastle head as is usual, but the drive, a vertical two-cylinder engine, was situated under the forecastle head on main deck level. It was remotely controlled by extended rods on the forecastle head. This was a powerful machine, and the horizontal shaft from the engine drove a vertical shaft through bevel gears. The vertical shaft passed through a gland and bearing in the forecastle head deck, and at the head of the shaft was a bronze worm which in turn drove the main gear wheel of the windlass. The worm was housed in a steel casing with a door for inspection and lubrication.

When the new crew joined the ship at Purfleet, in July 1945, the 'chippy' was unfamiliar with the machine and used to lubricate the worm with oil from a squirt oil can. This proved disastrous because the heat generated by the gears was so great that the oil burst into flames. Thereafter a wooden spatula was used to literally throw clods of grease on to the revolving worm. Any excess grease that dropped off was used again. It sounds crude but it worked.

From the time that the *Iroquois* left Purfleet in July 1945, her windlass was used more frequently than that of the average foreign-going ship. Mooring and unmooring every odd day in the eastern Mediterranean, and at some ports using both anchors to moor, anchoring awaiting berths and finally using both anchors to steady the ship while towing the pipelines at Fuhayhil in Kuwait. As a result of this the teeth of the main drive worm had worn very thin, so it was decided to renew the worm before loading her final cargo at Kabda (near Abadan). This was attempted *en route* from Kuwait to the Shatt al Arab Lightship. While trying to fit the worm to the vertical drive shaft, it was found that the worm was oversize, so the engineers on board tried to reduce the diameter by filing, as no lathe was available. A gallant effort but not enough. Nevertheless, the windlass worked long enough to moor the ship at Kabda, but while unmooring and trying to weigh the port anchor, several teeth stripped off the bevel gears on the engine drive shaft under the forecastle head. The foredeck winch had to be used to heave the ropes, and then, by using wires, weigh the port anchor. Just to make things 'interesting', the anchor came up with its flukes in and had to remain this way all the way to Suez. It was during the NE monsoon, so the weather was good. At Suez Bay the broken bevel gear wheel and the teeth as well as the new worm gear were sent ashore. The bevel gear had the teeth stuck back on and served as a pattern for the gear to be cast. After about ten days all were returned to the ship, tested and all was well. It was believed that due to the oversize worm, stress was transferred to the vertical shaft through the deck bearing, and this caused the failure of the bevel gears.

# THE DEATH OF A GREAT SHIP

IN 1946, when she left Mina al Mahdi, the *Iroquois* first loaded a cargo at Kabda (Abadan) and started her journey home, stopping at Suez on 30 April for ten days while further repairs to her windlass were made. While lying at anchor, an oil slick was discovered around the ship. This was pin-pointed as coming from No. 6 port tank. The oil from this tank was discharged and distributed all around the ship (the ullages in every tank had increased due to the drop in temperature since loading), and a partly filled tank took much of the load. It was not possible to keep the ship perfectly upright, but the 1st Officer did a pretty good job. As one can imagine, the tank was in a sticky, dirty state, and there were no tank-cleaning facilities. The section of the tank in the way of the leak was thoroughly cleaned, the hole plugged and a large cement box put over it. Success again! The previously distributed cargo was then returned to No. 6 tank and all was well. While lying at anchor the ships D/F equipment (Radio Direction Finder) was re-calibrated, using the ship's motor lifeboat and emergency lifeboat radio. She was east-bound in the Arabian Sea *en route* to Suez, when, during breakfast, about 8.30, the main engines stopped, and the fireman descended on to the midships saloon saying that there was water pouring into the stokehold and that the ship might sink! The truth was that a small hole had appeared in the starboard hull plating about twelve feet below the water-line. The 4th Engineer with all good intentions tried to plug it with a piece of wood, but that only made the hole larger. To remedy the situation the 1st Officer suggested 'fishing a bolt'.

## FISHING A BOLT

A fishbolt is about 9″ long and ¾″ diameter. At each end of the bolt (above the hexagon head and below the thread) is a lug with a hole, into which is threaded a light wire grommet. These bolts are generally used for plugging holes in the ship's hull when rivets have been 'sprung'. The wire grommets are used to attach a messenger to the thread end, and a lowering line is attached to the head of the bolt. Any washer of suitable size from 3″ to 10″ could be slotted over the thread together with suitable packing. The idea is to send the messenger to the surface of the sea through the hole in the hull; recovering the messenger, and attaching it to the thread end of the bolt, then the whole assembly, bolt, washer and packing is gently lowered into the sea while the slack end of the messenger was taken up from within the hull. Hopefully the screwed end of the bolt would be guided into the hole in the hull, and the outside pressure of water would ram the bolt home and stop the leak.

This worked well on the *Iroquois*. The 1st Officer climbed up the stringers in the stokehold, and pushed a suitable piece of wood through the hole with a length of marline attached to it, to float to the surface. The 2nd Officer, Joe Burrowdale, went down the ship's side on a ladder to pick up the piece of wood, but it had drifted too far away to retrieve it, so he had to swim to reach it. All to no avail—the messenger had parted. The exercise was repeated and this time they were successful. The messenger was attached to the bolt, a 9″ washer and rubber packing (this prevented the washer from slipping off the bolt). The whole assembly was gently lowered in to the sea, with a length of halyard attached to the grommet in the head of the bolt, and the 1st Officer recovered the slack messenger into the stokehole. As soon as the bolt entered the hole it shot home with a thump. A strongback complete with washer and nut secured the whole assembly from the inside. During this period, of course, the starboard boilers were shut down and the bilge pump was working throughout. No further damage was done, but it was a clear indication of the thickness of the hull plating, and more of this trouble appeared in Suez Bay.

These delays caused her to leave Suez on 12 May, passing Gibraltar on 25 May. The voyage was smooth and uneventful except for the last forty-eight hours, when off the Portuguese coast, the *Iroquois* ran into thick fog.

The Master took the ship in close to the land, trying to sight Cape Finisterre. They heard the fog signal and saw the beam of the light, altered course from Cape Villano, and were so close that the light appeared above them. Needless to say they pulled out quickly. Approaching Ushant (West France) the deep-sea sounding machine was in operation every thirty minutes. This was quite a skilled job with the ship moving, knowing when the 'lead' had touched bottom, then the task of having to heave the whole lot in again, then taking the sounding tube and 'arming' it to the bridge. A good 'line of soundings' was run, and the Master seemed quite happy with the ship's position. They heard Ushant's fog signal, but were unable to see the light, so a course was set for Eddystone Rock. At 6 a.m. 30 May, just after sunrise, the fog lifted and there was Eddystone fine on the starboard bow.

She sailed on to Devonport, arriving there on the same day. After discharging the cargo she sailed for the Clyde, arriving there on 4 June. During her stay on the Clyde she was shunted around a few times, in and out of dry dock, where she was surveyed. In this survey it was stated that her engines were still in perfect working condition, but her plating had corroded down to three-sixteenths of an inch in places. She eventually found a permanent berth at the Dalmuir Basin, where prospective buyers viewed her. Eventually British Iron and Steel (Salvage) bought her and she left the Clyde on 24 January 1947 for her last voyage, arriving at Troon in Scotland on 12 February to be broken up by Belgian ship-breakers W.H. Arnott Young. This was felt by some people to be a sad end to a famous ship that had served twice in time of war, three oceans as well as many seas and rivers.

# ABBREVIATIONS

| | | | |
|---|---|---|---|
| Abad | Abadan | Alex | Alexandria |
| Alg | Algiers | Avon | Avonmouth |
| Balb | Balboa | Barry | Barry Island |
| Baton R. | Baton Rouge | Bchy | Beachy Head |
| Belf | Belfast | Berm | Bermuda |
| Bolt | Bolt Head | Bsbte | Brunsbuttel |
| Bxm | Brixham | Bzta | Binzerta |
| Carpi | Caripito | Casa | Casablanca |
| Cpn | Copenhagen | Crist | Cristobal |
| Cstza | Constantza | | |
| Dela | Delaware | Dov | Dover |
| Dss | Dungeness | Dub | Dublin |
| Dunnet | Dunnet Head | | |
| Estham | Eastham | Els | Elsinore |
| Fal | Falmouth | Flam | Flamborough Head |
| Fran | San Francisco | | |
| Galv | Galveston | Gbg | Gothenberg |
| Gib | Gibralta | Glas | Glasgow |
| Graves | Gravesend | Green | Greenock |
| Guant B | Guantanamo Bay | | |
| Hal | Halifax | Hamp R. | Hampton Roads |
| Houst | Houston | | |
| Inish | Inishtrahull | Istan | Istanbul |
| IW | Isle of Wight | | |
| Key W | Key West | | |
| Liv | Liverpool | Liz | Lizard Point |
| Los | Los Angeles | Lo | London |
| Mbro | Middlesborough | Mchr | Manchester |
| Meth R. | Methane Roads | Milfd H | Milford Haven |
| Mlt | Malta | | |
| Nant | Nantucket Sound | N. Fore | North Fore Light |
| Nflk | Norfolk | N.O. | New Orleans |

| | | | |
|---|---|---|---|
| NWtg | Nieuwe Waterweg | N.Y. | New York |
| Nybg | Nykobing | | |
| Oxelo | Oxelosund | | |
| P.Arth | Port Arthur | P.Hbr | Pearl Harbour |
| Pir | Pireas | Ply | Plymouth |
| Ptld B | Portland Bill | Pwle | Prawle Point |
| Qtn | Queenstown | | |
| Ross | Rosslare | Runc | Runcorn |
| Sci | Scilly Isles | Shlds | North Shields |
| Skaw | Skaw Taing | Snd | Southend |
| Sou | Southampton | Spurn | Spurn Head |
| Thames H | Thames Haven | Torb | Torbay |
| Trin | Trinidad | Trip | Tripoli |
| Usht | Ushant | | |
| Vent | Ventnor | | |
| Walm | Walmer | | |

YEAR 1907/08 NEW 29/6/1907

OCT 21 21 22 | NOV 7 8 22 23 26 27 28 30 | DEC 2
Belf 32 Barry I 7 Barry I 5 Naut 16 NY 18 NY 20 NY 20 Puile 2 Dov 1 Lo 1 Lo(c) 29 Lo 31

2 3 4 18 31 | JAN 3 7 7 8 9 11 13 13 14
Snd 31 Dov 1 Puile 2 Phil 19 Phil 23 | 1908 | NY 16 NY 24 Liz 2 Sou 1 Lo 1 Lo(c) 33 Puile 2 Lo 1 Liz 2

28 | FEB | 11/20 15/3 17/1 22/28 24/1 24/2 24/3 25/2 26/3 28/17 28/4
NY 22 NY 31/1 Puile 15/2 Lo 16/2 Lo(c) 22/2 Lo (N.Fore) 23/2 23/2 (IW) (Liz) 24/2 Barry 25/2 Ross 28/2 Barry 27/2

FEB 29/23 | MARCH | 3/6 TOWING NAVAHOE 4/5 7/37 20/20 23/22 | APRIL | 2/18 3/17 10/22
Belf 28/2 Belf 7/3 (Brow) 3/3 H/3 51N 16W Naut 19/3 NY 21/3 NY 27/3 NY 27/3 Brow 10/14

11/3 13/3 13/4 16/24 20/6 20/1 21/3 21/5 25/2 30/23 | MAY | 5/23 6/19
Liz 11/4 Ross 12/4 Lo 13/4 Lo(c) 15/4 Sci 20/4 Lo 18/4 Liz 20/1 (Brow) 21/4 24/4 47N 20W Naut 4/5 NY 5/5

19/22 20/20 21/24 23/26 23/26 25/2 25/25 26/1 28/19 30/1
NY(c) 8/5 NY 9/5 17/5 45N 36W Liz 23/5 (Brow) 22/5 (N Fore) 23/5 25/5 Lo 25/5 Lo(c) 28/5 Lo 29/5

30/1 | JUNE | 1/5 2/5 13/20 15/25 | JULY | 1/22 2/30 6/10 7/42
(N Fore) 29/5 Liz 1/6 (Brow) 2/6 Naut 12/6 NY 13/9 NY 14/10 NY 3/7 (Brow) 5/7 Puile 7/7

7/3 7/3 8/1 9/1 15/29 16/1 16/1 17/1 17/1 17/2 18/3
(Liz) 7/7 Liz 7/7 N Fore 8/7 Lo 9/7 Lo(c) 14/7 Lo 15/7 N Fore 15/7 16/7 Dov 16/7 (IW) 17/7 Puile 17/7

| SHIPS NAME | NET TONNAGE | PORT OF REGISTRY | CAPTAIN |
|---|---|---|---|
| IROQUOIS (BRIT.) | 5772 | BELFAST | J.D. SCOTT 23/10/07 |

YEAR
1903/09

18/3 20/10 30/20 31/20 | AUG | 12/23 12/28 15/27 17/28 18/1
(Liz) 17/7 (Brow) 19/7 (Naut) 29/7 NY 30/7 NY 3/8 NY 4/8 9/8 42N 46W 1W 17/8 (N Fore) 18/8

19/1 22/22 25/11 | SEPT | 8/30 21/29 20/30 23/31 24/25 25/21 26/1
Lo 18/8 Lo 22/8 (Brow) 25/8 NY 7/9 18/9 48N 41W NY 11/9 (Brow) 23/7 Liz 24/9 1W 24/9 Lo 26/9

30/26 30/29 | OCT | 7/6 8/5 22/20 23/20 | NOV | 4/19 9/7 10/2
(N Fore) 30/9 Lo 30/9 Shlds 6/10 (Bel) 7/10 Naut 21/10 NY 22/10 NY 26/10 (Brow) 9/11 Liz 9/11

10/2 11/25 12/1 14/25 17/1 17/1 17/2 18/2 18/2 20/5 | DEC | 3/18
Liz 10/11 Dov 11/11 Lo 11/11 Lo(c) 14/11 Lo 16/11 (N Fore) 16/11 1W 16/11 Liz 17/11 18/11 Brow 19/11 NY 2/12

15/29 21/25 21/7 22/2 22/26 23/1 29/25 31/24 | JAN | 1/1
NY 4/12 Liz 21/12 (Brow) 20/12 1W 21/12 Dov 22/12 Lo 1/12 Lo(c) 28/12 Lo 31/12 | 1909 | (N Fore) 31/12

1/1 2/2 2/3 4/3 4/7 14/16 16/16 | FEB | 5/18 9/28 9/1
1W 1/1 Liz 2/1 Sci 2/1 Liz 2/1 (Brow) 4/1 Naut 13/1 NY 15/1 Dela 26/1 Phila 9/2 1W 9/2

10/1 11/1 13/26 15/1 15/2 15/27 15/28 16/2 16/2 | MARCH | 2/24
(N Fore) 10/20 Lo 10/2 Lo(c) 13/2 Lo 14/2 1W 14/2 Belf 15/2 (Liz) 15/2 Phila 15/2 Liz 16/2 Naut 1/5

4/7 2/22 18/20 20/27 23/2 24/1 25/1 27/35 29/1 29/2
NY 8/3 Lo 8/3 NY 9/3 (Liz) 22/3 (1W) 22/3 (N Fore) 23/3 Lo 24/3 Lo(c) 26/3 Lo 28/3 Snd 28/3

| SHIPS NAME | NET TONNAGE | PORT OF REGISTRY | CAPTAIN |
|---|---|---|---|
| TOWING BARGE NAVAHOE | 5772 | BELFAST | J. D. SCOTT |
| IROQUOIS (BRIT.) | | | |

YEAR
1909/10

29/2 29/3 30/2 30/2 30/3 30/3 | APRIL | 14/26 15/20
(N Fore) 27/3 (1W) 29/3 Pwle 29/3 (Belt) 29/3 Liz 30/3 Sci 30/3 Nant 13/4 NY 14/4

MAY | 4/32 27/4 8/22 11/31 12/1 13/1 15/24 17/34 13/2 18/32
NY 24/4 29/4 40N 65W 30/4 41N 61W Liz 11/5 (N Fore) 12/5 Lo 12/5 Lo(C) 15/5 Lo 17/5 1W 18/5 (Belt) 18/5

18/32 19/3 20/7 31/29 | JUNE | 2/26 15/34 16/36 18/36 9/25 21/1
Liz 18/5 Liz 19/5 (Brow) 19/5 Nant 30/5 NY 1/6 NY 4/6 NY 6/6 (Brow) 18/6 (Belt) Head 19/6 Lo 21/6

23/6 24/1 26/8 | JULY | 14/7 15/7 24/22 26/27 | AUG | 20/27 24/5
Lo 23/6 Sud 23/6 Shlds 25/6 Shlds 13/7 Dunnet 14/7 Nant 23/7 NY 25/7 NY 13/8 Brow 23/8

25/37 26/1 28/1 | SEPT | 1/33 2/1 2/2 2/3 2/25 3/3 4/29 11/22
(Liz) 25/8 Thames H 26/8 Lo 28/8 Lo(C) 31/8 Lo 1/9 (1W) 1/9 Belt 2/8 Liz 2/9 2/9 Brow 4/9 11/9

13/28 13/28 29/20 | OCT | 2/20 5/44 6/2 7/1 9/24 22/31 25/29
Nant 11/9 NY 12/9 NY 20/9 NY 22/9 (Liz) 5/10 iW 6/10 Thames H 7/10 Lo 9/10 Lo(C) 22/10 (Liz) 25/10

25/1 26/4 27/29 | NOV | 5/18 6/26 18/21 23/35 25/3 29/29 29/6
Lo 23/10 Liz 25/10 (Brow) 27/10 Nant 4/11 NY 5/11 NY 9/11 (Brow) 23/11 Avon 24/11 (Brow 29/11 Avon 27/11

DEC | 10/18 11/20 28/32 28/33 29/2 30/2 30/2 31/1 | JAN | 3/26 4/19
Nant 9/12 NY 10/12 NY 17/12 (Brow) 28/12 (Belt) 29/12 1W 29/12 Pwle 29/12 Lo 30/12 | 1910 | Lo(C) 3/1 Lo 4/1

| SHIPS NAME | NET TONNAGE | PORT OF REGISTRY | CAPTAIN |
|---|---|---|---|
| TOWING BARGE NAVAHOE | 5772 | BELFAST | J D SCOTT |
| IROQUOIS (BRIT.) | | | |

YEAR
1910

5/30 7/2 7/17 8/3 10/7 21/24 24/28 25/30 | FEB | 8/31 12/27

(N Fore) 3/1 (1W) 6/1 Liz 7/1 8/1 (Brow) 9/1 16/1 48N 35W Naut 23/1 NY 24/1 NY 27/1 NY 30/1

12.50 PM

12/24 14/23 (wireless) 14/24 wireless 15/2 16/1 21/27 23/1 24/2 25/3

5/2 41N 50W 13/2 130m NW Liz 14/2 Abm Ptld Vent 14/2 Lo 15/2 Lo(c) 21/2 Lo 22/2 Belvy 23/2 Liz 24/2

26/2 | MARCH | 14/28 26/28 29/27 | APRIL | 1/28 2/26 5/33 6/27 7/1 7/1

25/2 110m W NY 13/3 NY 16/3 NY 18/3 30/3 1W 1/4 Lo 2/4 Lo(c) 5/4 Lo 6/4 Walm 6/4 Dov 6/4

7/23 8/23 (Brow) 19/30 21/26 | MAY | 3/31 5/23 6/2 7/1 10/38 11/29

7/4 Nr Btld B 7/4 40mW Naut 18/4 NY 19/4 NY 22/4 5/5 Abm (Belt) Dov 6/5 Lo 6/5 Lo(c) 10/5 Lo 11/5

11/29 12/24 12/1 13/3 13/3 14/24 wireless 24/34 24/24 | JUNE | 7/28 8/28

Snd 11/5 11/5 Abm Ptld B Dov 11/5 Prole 12/5 Liz 12/5 14/5 Naut 23/5 16/5 48N 33W NY 24/5 NY 27/5

8/24 wireless 10/23 10/4 11/23 13/1 16/1 17/24 18/27 18/27 20/2

4/6 46N 36W 10/6 20mW Sci 10/6 10/6 80mE Lo 12/6 Lo 16/6 Lo(c) 15/6 Lo 18/6 Snd 18/6 Walm 18/6

20/24 21/24 wireless | JULY | 2/25 14/29 19/33 20/23 wireless 21/22 22/1 22/25 29/1

19/6 26/6 Belt Naut 1/7 NY 3/7 NY 8/7 20/7 50mW Liz 21/7 Thamesh 22/7 Lo 22/7 Lo 28/7

29/1 30/9 | AUG | 1/11 15/33 15/10 27/26 | SEPT | 1/26 7/29 10/20

Snd 28/7 Ham 29/7 Mbro 30/7 Dunnet 15/8 Mbro 13/8 Dela 26/8 NY 27/8 NY 30/8 Dela 31/8

| SHIPS NAME | NET TONNAGE | PORT OF REGISTRY | CAPTAIN |
|---|---|---|---|
| TOWING BARGE NAVAHOE | 5772 | BELFAST | J D SCOTT |
| IROQUOIS (BRIT.) | | | |

YEAR
1910/11

13/24 13/24 wireless 15/1 20/1 20/1 20/1 20/24 21/3 22/23
12/9 110m W 14/9 90m E Liz Lo 19/9 Snd 19/9 Walm 19/9 Dov 19/9 20/9 15m E Liz 20/9 21/9 120m SW

22/23 | OCT | 1/20 3/29 18/25 18/33 20/3 20/35 21/21 22/1
24/9 49N 34W Nant 30/9 NY 2/10 14/10 10.48N 11.40W NY 7/10 Liz 20/10 Pwle 20/10 Dov 21/10 Lo 21/10

29/25 31/36 | NOV | 1/1 1/1 2/1 2/30 3/4 3/24 16/30 18/25
Lo 23/10 Snd 31/10 Walm 31/10 Dov 31/10 Lo 31/10 Liz 2/11 Sci 2/11 3/11 133m S Nant 15/11 NY 17/11

29/33 | DEC | 2/25 5/24 6/38 7/1 8/24 8/1 anchored 12/25 16/1 16/1 15/1
NY 18/11 NY 20/11 24/11 100m E IW 6/12 Dov 6/12 Lo 6/12 Lo 7/12 Lo 10/12 Lo 11/12 Snd 14/12 Walm 14/12

10/25 17/2 20/40 20/25 20/25 21/6 31/20 | JAN | 2/28 12/20
16/12 Abm Liz Liz 16/12 Torr 20/12 Fal 19/12 Belf 20/12 Inish 20/12 Nant 30/12 | 1911 | NY 1/1 NY 31/12

16/24 17/1 19/1 21/28 23/1 23/5 | FEB | 4/20 15/30 16/25 wireless
15/12 70m E Liz ThamesH 16/1 Lo 18/1 Lo 20/1 Lo 21/1 Liz 22/1 60m W Liz NY 3/2 NY 5/2 15/2 20m S

17/3 20/30 20/6 21/6 23/5 | MARCH | 24/1 25/1 27/24 29/1
Avon 16/2 Avon 19/2 Barry I 19/2 Dub 20/2 Dub 22/2 ThamesH 24/3 Lo 25/3 Lo 27/3 Lo 28/3

29/1 29/19 wireless 29/25 30/25 | APRIL | 5/28 5/28 18/35 19/26 | MAY | 3/26
Dov 28/3 Dss 28/3 Ptld B 29/3 Belf 4/4 Inish 4/4 Nant 17/4 NY 18/4 NY 24/4

| SHIPS NAME | NET TONNAGE | PORT OF REGISTRY | CAPTAIN |
|---|---|---|---|
| | | | J.D. SCOTT |
| TOWING BARGE NAVAHOE | 5772 | BELFAST | |
| IROQUOIS (BRIT.) | | | |

YEAR
1911/12

8/4 9/1 12/23 13/1 13/21 13/5 25/5 JUNE 6/26 7/18 20/23
Pwle 8/5 Lo 9/5 Lo 11/5 Lo 12/5 Dov 13/5 Belf 16/5 Belf 23/5 25/5 90m W Brow Nant 5/6 NY 6/6 NY 9/6

21/32 26/2 30/23 30/1 30/2 JULY 1/2 1/22 3/6 14/18 26/24 AUG 1/2
NY 11/6 Dov 25/6 Lo 29/6 Lo 29/6 Dov 30/6 Bchy 30/6 1/7 50m SE Sci 1/7 NY 13/7 NY 13/7 Pwle 1/8

2/26 Collision 1/21 9/36 11/3 11/25 12/28 SEPT 1/28 3/28 6/20 11/9
Lo 2/8 Mig 28/7 Lo 9/8 Liz 10/8 11/8 85m W Liz 11/8 100m SE NY 22/8 NY 25/8 NY 28/8 Dov 11/9

12/1 13/25 16/21 18/23 wireless 29/24 wireless OCT 2/29 16/27 17/32 19/34 20/32
Lo 11/9 Lo 12/9 Lo 16/9 18/9 85m W Liz 18/9 130m SW NY 1/10 NY 4/10 NY 6/10 Liz 19/10 Dss 20/10

22/35 23/1 27/35 28/1 30/4 NOV 8/26 14/27 15/33 16/26
Lo 21/10 Lo 21/10 Lo 26/10 Lo 27/10 Pwle 29/10 4/11 50N 28W 7/11 48N 39W Nant 14/11 NY 15/11

28/22 28/31 28/30 DEC 4/34 5/28 8/34 12/2 14/25 15/27 wireless 22/28
NY 16/11 NY 17/11 NY 19/11 Bchy 4/12 Lo 4/12 Lo 8/12 IW 12/12 Liz 13/12 13/12 130m SE 18/12 50N 27W

27/25 'NAVAHOE' JAN 3/16 5/20 18/18 18/34 25/3 25/21 26/19 27/1
20/12 49N 33W 1912 PArth 2/1 NY 2/1 NY 9/1 NY 11/1 Sci 25/1 Liz 25/1 Bchy 26/1 Lo 27/1

FEB 1/1 3/3 2/24 16/18 17/18 MARCH 5/28 7/17 9/23 wireless 11/3
Lo 30/1 Liz 2/2 3/2 120m W Nant 15/2 NY 16/2 NY 21/2 NY 24/2 9/5 140m SE Bchy 11/3

| SHIPS NAME | NET TONNAGE | PORT OF REGISTRY | CAPTAIN |
|---|---|---|---|
| | | | J.A. COLLIE 16/9/1911 |
| TOWING BARGE NAVAHOE | 5772 | BELFAST | J.D. SCOTT 26/10/1911 |
| IROQUOIS (BRIT.) | | | |

YEAR
1912/13

12/1 15/17 16/1 18/24 APRIL 4/6 17/16 20/18 24/36 25/21 26/1
Lo 11/3 Lo 15/3 IW 16/3 18/3 120m W Liz Nant 3/4 NY 5/4 NY 8/4 Sci 24/4 IW 25/4 Lo 26/4

30/41 MAY 1/36 2/1 2/2 17/18 18/16 28/42 JUNE 4/30 6/3 7/1 8/1
Lo 30/4 Lo 1/5 Snd 1/5 Dov 1/5 Nant 16/5 NY 17/5 NY 18/5 NY 22/5 Pwle 6/6 Dov 7/6 Lo 7/6

11/24 11/44 12/1 12/1 13/3 13/3 28/18 JULY 1/20 10/26 17/30 18/42
Lo 10/6 Lo 11/6 Snd 11/6 Walm 11/6 Liz 12/6 Sci 13/6 Nant 27/6 NY 29/6 NY 29/6 NY 3/7 Pwle 18/7

19/2 20/7 23/24 24/2 24/41 25/28 AUG 9/19 10/25 22/20 24/33 24/25
Bchy 19/7 Lo 20/7 Lo 22/7 Dov 24/7 IW 24/7 Sci 25/7 Nant 8/8 NY 9/8 NY 10/8 NY 13/8 14/8 190m E

27/23 wireless 28/3 29/19 31/19 SEPT 2/41 2/29 3/2 3/24 wireless 4/23
26/8 140m SW Pwle 28/8 Lo 29/8 Lo 31/8 Dss 2/9 Snd 2/9 PtldB 3/9 3/9 90m S Liz 4/9

19/20 OCT 2/25 8/29 11/2 11/26 wireless 12/1 12/1 14/1 19/1 19/1
NY 18/9 NY 23/9 NY 26/9 Liz 10/10 10/10 80m E Bchy 11/10 Dov 11/10 Lo 13/10 Lo 18/10 Snd 18/10

19/26 21/5 22/25 NOV 7/18 20/20 25/38 26/3 27/28 30/1 DEC 2/11
IW 19/10 Sci 20/10, 20/10 NY 6/11 NY 11/11 Sci 25/11 Liz 25/11 Lo 27/11 Lo 29/11 Flam 2/12

2/11 4/6 13/18 JAN 1/18 2/25 14/29 22/20 22/19 23/19 23/19
Shlds 3/12 Shlds 11/12 Dunnet 12/12 1913 Nant 31/4 NY 1/1 NY 2/1 NY 8/1 Liz 2/1 Lo 23/1 Lo 28/1

| SHIPS NAME | NET TONNAGE | PORT OF REGISTRY | CAPTAIN |
|---|---|---|---|
| TOWING BARGE NAVAHOE | 5772 | BELFAST | J.D. SCOTT |
| IROQUOIS (BRIT.) | | | |

YEAR
1913

28/33 wireless 31/25 wireless | FEB | 18/29 19/26 | MARCH | 4/28 7/20 8/36
Snd 28/1 29/4 15m SE Brow 31/1 100m S Liz Naut 17/2 Dela 18/2 NY 21/2 NY 24/2 Dela 25/2

(Brow) 11/2 12/1 13/1 15/24 17/1 anchored 7/1 18/2 18/11 19/23 20/3
Pwle 11/3 Dov 12/3 Lo 12/3 Lo(c) 14/3 Lo 15/3 Snd 16/3 Dov 17/3 I W 18/3 18/3 50m E Liz Sci 19/3

20/24 wireless 20/25 (wireless) | APRIL | 5/20 7/31 25/26 30/30 | MAY | 5/24 5/5
19/3 150m SE 20/3 130m SW Naut 4/4 NY 5/4 NY 12/45 NY 21/4 5/5 130m SE Pwle 5/5

6/44 9/24 10/1 10/1 10/2 12/5 12/24 wireless 27/38 | JUNE | 9/31 10/32
Lo 6/5 Lo(c) 9/5 Lo 9/5 Snd 9/5 Bchy 10/5 Pwle 10/5 11/5 120m SE NY 26/5 NY 29/5 Dela 30/5

12/33 13/3 14/1 18/24 14/44 19/1 20/4 21/24 wireless | JULY | 5/27 16/28
Sci 12/6 I W 13/6 Lo 14/6 Lo(c) 17/6 I W 19/6 Lo 18/6 Sci 20/6 20/6 175m W Phil 4/7 Phil(c) 7/7

21/37 22/24 23/4 22/23 wireless 24/1 25/1 28/1 28/2 29/7
Dela 9/7 21/7 170m SW Sci 22/7 23/7 Liz Snd 24/7 Lo 24/7 Lo 27/7 Snd 27/7 Flam 28/7

30/6 | AUG | 18/1 19/6 | SEPT | 2/30 17/31 20/23 22/2
Shlds 17/8 Shlds 17/8 Dunnet 18/8 NY 1/9 NY 6/9 19/9 140m SE Bolt Dov 21/9

22/23 23/1 25/24 26/32 27/1 27/2 27/2 29/5 29/24
21/9 100m E Lo 22/9 Lo(c) 25/9 Lo 26/9 Snd 26/9 Dov 26/9 Bchy 26/9 Liz 27/9 28/9 100m S

| SHIPS NAME | NET TONNAGE | PORT OF REGISTRY | CAPTAIN |
|---|---|---|---|
| TOWING BARGE NAVAHOE | 5772 | BELFAST | J. D. SCOTT |
| IROQUOIS (BRIT.) | | | |

YEAR
1913/14

30/24 wireless | OCT | 10/24 10/30 22/28 27/23 wireless 28/43 29/33 30/29 | NOV | 3/42
28/9 100m SW Nant 9/10 NY 10/10 NY 11/10 27/10 215m SW Sci 28/10 IW 29/10 Lo 30/10 Lo(c) 1/11

4/1 (Brow) 4/2 4/44 5/3 6/23 wireless (Brow) 20/30 21/30 | DEC | 2/36 5/20
Lo 3/11 Bchy 4/11 IW 4/11 PHd B 4/11 5/11 140m W Liz Nant 19/11 NY 20/11 NY(c) 21/11 NY 23/11

8/24 wireless 9/40 10/1 13/24 15/1 15/2 15/23 20/6 29/26
7/12 220m W LandsE Bchy 9/12 Lo 10/12 Lo(c) 12/12 Lo 13/12 Dov 13/12 14/12 45m E LandsE Dunnet 19/12 NY 28/12

JAN | 13/36 17/26 19/2 20/1 23/21 26/24 Towing 'Navahoe' 27/26 | FEB | 12/19
1914 | NY 1/1 16/1 105m SW Dov 19/1 Lo 19/1 Lo 23/1 25/1 110m SW Brow 26/1 130m SW Brow Nant 11/2

13/29 27/26 | MARCH | 4/32 5/23 (wireless) 6/24 (wireless) 7/1 11/24 12/36
NY 12/2 NY(c) 6/2 NY 18/2 5/3 180m W LandsE 5/3 120m SEq Brow Lo 7/3 Lo(c) 10/3 Lo 13/3

13/1 13/2 14/31 17/6 (wireless) | APRIL | 3/20 4/29 20/32 23/35 28/1
Walm 12/3 Dov 12/3 Liz 14/3 16/3 130m SW Brow Nant 2/4 NY 3/4 NY 8/4 Lo 23/4 Lo 27/4

28/37 28/48 29/2 29/23 (wireless) | MAY | 2/25 (wireless) 14/26 25/30 28/33
Dss 28/4 Dss 28/4 Bchy 28/4 29/4 60m E 30/4 140m SE NY 13/5 NY 15/5 NY 16/5

29/15 (wireless) 30/26 (wireless) | JUNE | 1/34 1/1 3/28 5/1 5/2 5/2 6/31 6/4
28/5 164m SW Brow 30/5 LandsE Vent 30/5 Lo 30/5 Lo(c) 3/6 Lo 4/6 Dov 5/6 Bchy 5/6 Vent 5/6 Sci 6/6

| SHIPS NAME | NET TONNAGE | PORT OF REGISTRY | CAPTAIN |
|---|---|---|---|
| TOWING BARGE NAVAHOE | 5772 | BELFAST | J.D. SCOTT |
| IROQUOIS (BRIT.) | | | |

| YEAR |
|---|
| 1914 \| 15 \| 16 |

23/31 30/31 | JULY | 9/32 10/7 11/2 15/4 16/5 17/6 17/33 31/32
NY 20/6 NY 25/6 7/7 135m SW Pwle 9/7 Lo 10/7 Lo 14/7 IW 15/7 Pwle 15/7 Liz 15/7 NY 29/7

AUG | 4/19 30/4 | OCT | 1/2 2/2 22/18 | NOV | 9/7 10/4 11/9 20/5 | JAN | 9/15
NY 2/8 Pwle 29/9 Snd 30/9 Lo 30/9 NY 20/10 Liz 7/11 Snd 9/11 Lo 9/11 Liv 18/11 | 1915 | NY 7/1

FEB | 1/3 2/2 | MARCH | 2/17 22/2 | APRIL | 2/25 17/17 | MAY | 3/2 7/2 8/3 25/17
Dss 31/1 Lo 1/2 NY 25/2 Lo 20/3 NY 10/4 NY 15/4 Lo 2/5 Lo 6/5 Dov 7/5 NY 23/5

31/21 | JUNE | 12/3 14/2 18/2 18/3 19/4 | JULY | 2/17 5/25 19/2 Anchor 23/2 24/2
NY 28/5 Dov 11/6 Lo 12/6 Lo 17/6 Snd 17/6 Dov 17/6 NY 30/6 NY 3/2 Lo 18/7 Lo 22/7 Lo 22/7

24/4 | AUG | 9/21 12/18 27/2 | SEPT. | 7/2 7/2 8/3 28/19 | OCT | 23/15
Dss 23/7 NY 6/8 NY 10/8 Lo 26/8 Lo 6/9 Snd 6/9 Dov 6/9 Colon 26/9 Crist 9/10

27/17 13/4 13/2 18/2 18/3 Anchored 20/2 22/4 DEC 4/5 22/4 29/3 30/2
Sabine 27/10 Dov 10/11 Lo 12/11 Lo 17/11 Snd 17/11 Snd 13/11 Dov 19/3 NY 2/12 NY 10/2 Dov 2/5 Lo 28/12

JAN | 6/2 26/15 | MARCH | 8/17 24/3 25/3 27/3 29/2 29/2 31/2
1916 | Lo 5/1 NY 24/12 NY 6/3 Bchy — 1 — Dss — 1 — Dov — 1 — Lo 27/3 ThamesH 28/3 ThamesH 30/3

APRIL | 1/2 4/2 8/6 19/7 | MAY | 8/19 8/4 9/4 10/2 15/3
Lo 31/3 Dov — 1 — Dss — 1 — NY 17/4 NY 21/4 Liz — 1 — Bchy — 1 — Lo 9/5 Lo 13/5

| SHIPS NAME | NET TONNAGE | PORT OF REGISTRY | CAPTAIN |
|---|---|---|---|
| | | | J D SCOTT |
| TOWING BARGE NAVAHOE | 5772 | BELFAST | E.C. THDWAY 1/2/15 |
| | | | J.D. SCOTT 23/3/15 |
| IROQUOIS (BRIT.) | | | |

YEAR
1916/17

17/4 | JUNE | 1/17 6/19 21/4 22/3 23/4 24/2 28/2 28/3 29/3
1W — 1 —— NY 20/5 NY 4/6 Liz — 1 — Bchy — 1 — Dov — 1 — Lo 23/6 Lo 27/6 Snd 27/6 Bchy — 1 — Pwle ——

30/4 | JULY | 15/16 24/19 | AUG | 5/4 7/4 8/3 9/2 10/3 18/4
- 1 ——— NY 13/7 NY 22/7 —— Liz — 1 — Ply — 1 — Bchy — 1 — Snd 8/8 ThamesH 8/8 Bchy — 1 — PHdB

19/4 21/4 | SEPT | 4/16 21/15 23/4 25/4 26/3 | OCT | 2/3 2/3 5/2
— 1 — Liz — 1 ——— NY 1/9 NY 8/9 Sci — 1 — Bchy — 1 — Lo 25/9 Lo 30/9 Snd — 1 — Dov — 1 —

JAN | 3/22 9/22 Towing Barge 25/2 Towing Barge 27/1 29/1 | FEB | 3/2 7/2 26/16 | APRIL | 17/3 18/2
1917 | NY 1/1 NY 7/1 Bchy 24/1 Downs 25/1 Lo 27/1 Lo 1/2 Liz 6/2 NY 23/2 1W 16/4 Bchy 16/4

19/1 21/1 26/1 26/13 27/14 28/16 | MAY | 24/14 26/1 26/13 29/1 31/1
Dss 17/4 Lo 20/4 Lo 24/4 Snd 24/4 Pwle 26/4 Liz 26/4 Liz 23/5 Fal 24/5 Bchy 25/5 Lo 26/5 Lo 30/5

JUNE | 1/17 2/14 4/15 ON ADMIRALTY CHARTER 13 17 25 30 | JULY | 8 15 23
Downs 31/1 Pwle 1/6 Liz 1/6 NY NY Sabine Sabine Phil Phil Sabine

28 AUG 4 17 23 | SEPT | 6 8 11 12 22 28/14 | OCT | 12/14
Sabine Phil Phil P.Arth Mont Mont Hal Hal Sabine Sabine 30/9 Hal 8/10

16/8 Towing Navahoe 24/20 26/13 | NOV | 1/2 12/16 15/18 23/17 26/17 28/13
Hal 11/10 Key W 19/10 P. Arth 22/10 P. Arth 27/10 Hal 7/11 Hal 12/11 Key W 18/11 P. Arth 22/11 P. Arth 25/11

| SHIPS NAME | NET TONNAGE | PORT OF REGISTRY | CAPTAIN |
| --- | --- | --- | --- |
| | | | J D SCOTT |
| TOWING BARGE NAVAHOE | 5772 | BELFAST | |

IROQUOIS (BRIT.)

YEAR
1917/18/19

DEC 4/14 11/14 9/15 12/19 21/19 25 JAN 1 11 17 29
Key W 28/11 Hal 6/12 Hal 21/11 Phil 25/11 Phil 25/12 Sabine 1918 Sabine Hal Hal P. Arth

29 30 31 FEB 13 16 MARCH 2 6 17 21 31 APRIL 4 15 19
P. Arth Sabine Sabine Hal Hal Sabine Sabine Hal Hal Sabine Sabine Hal Hal

30 MAY 3 14 19 29 JUNE 1 11 19 22 JULY 12 19 25 AUG 4
Sabine Sabine Hal Hal Sabine Sabine Hal Hal NY NY Sabine Sabine Hal

15 23 25 SEPT 4 15 23 25 OCT 3 11 21 27 NOV 13 19
Hal Sabine Sabine Hal Hal Sabine Sabine Hal Hal Sabine Sabine Hal Hal

29 DEC 3 15 21 24 24 JAN 13/5 14/2 15/3 20/2 31/2 FEB 5/1
Sabine Sabine Hal Hal Phil Phil 1919 1 W 11/1 Snd 12/1 Thames H 14/1 Lo 17/1 Lo 29/1 Lo 4/2

Towing Barge
5/3 10/6 11/5 21/2 MARCH 20/27 Towing Navahoe 27/13 29/17 APRIL Towing Navahoe 12/14 15/6 17/5
Thames H (c) 4/2 1 W 8/2 Ply 8/2 Ply 20/2 NO 17/3 Baton R 22/3 NO 26/3 P. Eads 27/3 Liz 14/4 Lo 16/4

26/2 28/4 29/4 30/4 JUNE 4/24 6/28 23/3 24/3 25/4 30/2
Lo (c) 25/4 Lo 29/4 Snd 27/4 Dss 28/4 Sand K (P) 18/5 NO 1/5 Dov 22/6 Snd 22/6 Thames H 24/6 Lo 28/6

JULY 1/3 1/10 2/8 AUG 12/3 13/1 14/3 15/3 16/22 (wireless) SEPT 1/25
Lo 29/6 Flam 30/6 Mbro 1/7 Lo 11/8 Lo (c) 12/8 Lo 13/8 Pwle 14/8 15/8 (Lands E) NO 29/8

| SHIPS NAME | NET TONNAGE | PORT OF REGISTRY | CAPTAIN |
|---|---|---|---|
| | | | J. D. SCOTT |
| TOWING BARGE NAVAHOE | 5772 | BELFAST | S. W. SMITH 12/8/19 |
| IROQUOIS (BRIT.) | | | |

YEAR
1919/20

Anchored
17/21 OCT 2/3 3/3 6/5 7/4 13/5 16/5 27/27 29/10 NOV 11/30
NO 15/9 Liz 30/9 Dov 1/10 Downs 2/10 Downs 3/10 S Pit 11/10 Liz 15/10 NY 25/10 Hamp R 9/10 NY 8/10

21/5 22/2 DEC 3/11 3/12 4/3 8/3 11/1 13/4 15/4 JAN 2/21
Liz 20/11 Dov 21/11 Cux 23/11 Thames H —1— Lo 6/12 Lo(C) 10/12 Lo 11/12 I W 13/12 1920 NY 31/12

8/19 22/28 (wireless) 23/5 24/2 30/2 FEB 2/2 3/4 4/24 (wireless) MARCH 4/28
NY 6/1 21/1 (Lands E) I W 22/1 Lo 23/1 Lo(C) 29/1 Lo 31/1 Bchy 1/1 3/2 (Lands E NO 2/3

Towing Collision
20/21 23/7 23/23 24/23 25/2 25/23 29/3 29/4 30/8
P. Eads 2/3 Liz 22/3 Lands E 22/3 Fal 22/3 Lo 24/3 Graves 24/3 Lo 27/3 Snd 27/3 Mbro 28/3

MAY 17/2 17/3 18/4 19/5 28/18 JUNE 19/20 JULY 7/20 (wireless 9/3 13/3 14/3
Lo 15/5 Lo 16/5 Bchy 16/5 Liz 17/5 NY 26/5 Gulf 17/6 6/7 200m fr. Lands E Lo 8/7 Lo(C) 12/7 Lo 13/7

14/3 15/4 16/5 16/21 (wireless) 21/18 AUG 18/15 SEPT 3/23 7/21 (wireless)
Snd 13/7 Bchy 14/7 I W 14/7 14/7 Lands E Nflk 19/7 P. Arth 15/8 Sabine 16/8 6/9 (Lands E)

Towing
8/5 9/4 10/3 11/3 14/3 14/4 16/4 17/6 Oct 4/28
Liz 6/9 Dov 8/9 Thames H 9/9 Thames H 10/9 Lo(C) 13/9 Thames H (C) 13/9 Bchy 14/9 Liz 15/9 Phil 30/9

7/24 20/24 21/28 21/24 (wireless) 23/5 28/3 28/3 NOV 1/1
Phil 5/10 Rudy Is 5/10 Dela 6/10 20/10 (Valentia) Liz 22/10 Thames H 25/10 Lo 25/10 Lo(C) 30/10

| SHIPS NAME | NET TONNAGE | PORT OF REGISTRY | CAPTAIN |
|---|---|---|---|
| | | | S W SMITH |
| TOWING BARGE NAVAHOE | 5772 | BELFAST | J D SCOTT 6/12/1919 |
| IROQUOIS (BRIT.) | | | |

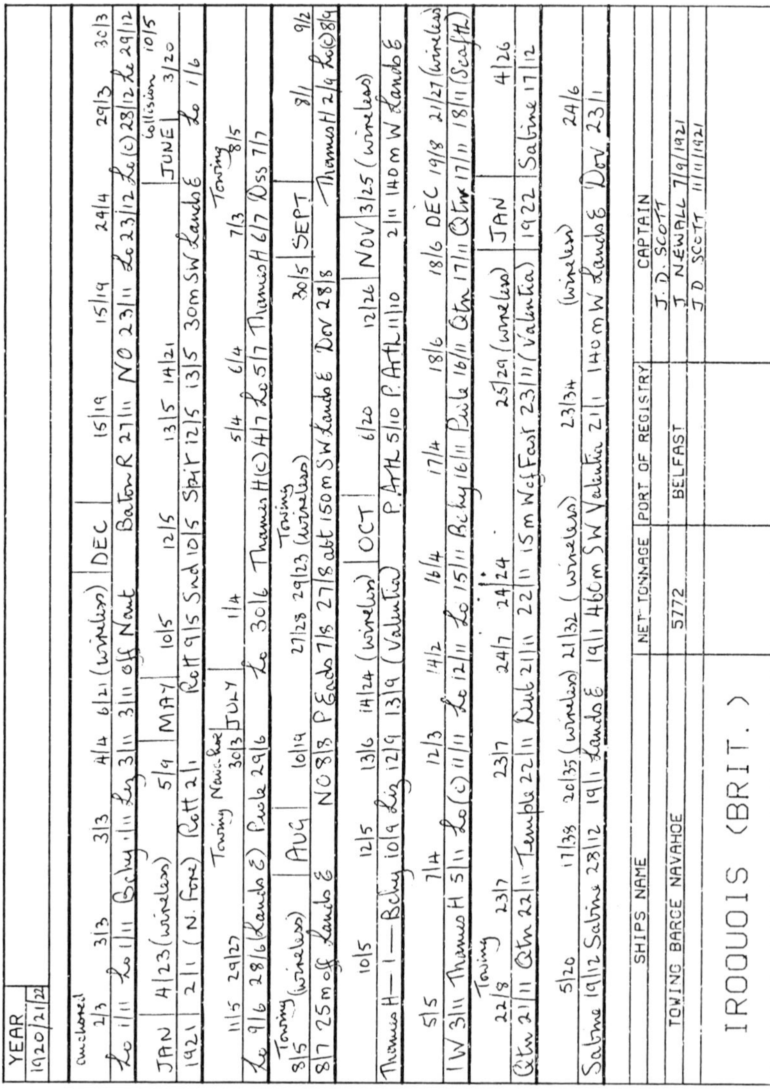

YEAR
1920/21/22

anchored
2/3 3/3 3/3 4/4 6/21 (wireless) DEC 15/19 15/19 24/4 29/3 30/3
Lo 1/11 Lo 1/11 Bchy 1/11 Liz 3/11 3/11 off Nant Baton R 27/11 NO 23/11 Lo 23/12 Lo(c) 28/12 Lo 29/12

JAN 4/23 (wireless) 5/9 MAY 10/5 12/5 13/5 14/21 JUNE collision 10/5 3/20
1921 2/1 (N. Fore) Rott 2/1 Rott 9/5 Snd 10/5 Spit 12/5 13/5 30m SW Lands E Lo 1/6

11/5 29/27 Towing Navahoe 30/3 JULY 1/4 5/4 6/4 7/3 Towing 8/5
Lo 9/6 28/6 (Lands E) Pule 29/6 Lo 30/6 Thames H(c) 4/7 Lo 5/7 Thames H 6/7 Dss 7/7

Towing 8/5 (wireless) AUG 10/19 27/28 29/23 Towing (wireless) 30/5 SEPT 8/1 9/2
8/7 25m off Lands E NO 8/8 P Eads 7/8 27/8 abt 150m SW Lands E Dov 28/8 Thames H 2/9 Lo(c) 8/9

10/5 12/5 13/6 14/24 (wireless) OCT 6/20 12/26 NOV 3/25 (wireless)
Thames H — 1 — Bchy 10/9 Liz 12/9 13/9 (Valentia) P. Arth 5/10 P. Arth 11/10 2/11 140m W Lands E

5/5 7/4 12/3 14/2 16/4 17/4 18/6 18/6 DEC 19/8 21/27 (wireless)
1W 3/11 Thames H 5/11 Lo(c) 11/11 Lo 12/11 Lo 15/11 Bchy 16/11 Pule 16/11 Qtn 17/11 Qtn 17/11 18/11 (Scaf'th)

Towing 22/8 23/7 23/7 24/7 24/24 25/29 (wireless) JAN 4/26
Qtn 21/11 Qtn 22/11 Temple 22/11 Dub 21/11 22/11 15m W of Fast 23/11 (Valentia) 1922 Sabine 17/12

5/20 17/38 20/35 (wireless) 21/32 (wireless) 23/34 (wireless) 24/6
Sabine 19/12 Sabine 28/12 19/1 Lands E 19/1 460m SW Valentia 21/1 140m W Lands E Dov 23/1

| SHIPS NAME | NET TONNAGE | PORT OF REGISTRY | CAPTAIN |
|---|---|---|---|
| | | | J. D. SCOTT |
| TOWING BARGE NAVAHOE | 5772 | BELFAST | J NEWALL 7/9/1921 |
| | | | J D SCOTT 11/11/1921 |
| IROQUOIS (BRIT.) | | | |

YEAR 1922/23

26/4 30/3 FEB 15/3 23/3 24/5 27/33 (wireless) MARCH 22/34
Thames H 25/1 Lo 29/1 Thames H(c) 14/2 Lo 22/2 Dss 22/2 26/2 (220m dist Valentia) Key W 20/3

APRIL 5/35 21/27 24/30 (wireless) 25/31 (wireless) 27/4 28/5 MAY 10/4
NO 23/3 Sandy K(p) 6/4 22/4 (41 22N 20W) 23/4 (Lands E) Dov 26/4 Thames H 27/4 Lo(c) 4/5

Towing Barge Navahoe
JUNE 12/19 12/6 13/30 (wireless) 15/3 (wireless) JULY 1/34 17/34 SEPT 5/37
RoH 8/6 Spit 11/6 11/6 200m E Lands E 12/6 (Lands E) Colon 29/6 Fran 14/7 Fran 21/8

5/37 11/27 OCT 2/3 (wireless) 3/7 4/4 6/4 10/12 11/11
S. Ed 23/8 Pan 8/9 30/9 350m W Lands E Liz 2/10 Dov 3/10 Thames H 5/10 Spurn 9/10 Hull 9/10

16/13 18/9 30/13 30/14 NOV 1/4 1/5 2/5 3/6 15/41
Flam 14/10 Shlds 16/10 Shlds 28/10 Flam 28/10 Thames H 30/10 Dov 31/10 IW 1/11 Pwle 1/11 NO 1/11

Towing Barge
DEC 21/33 (wireless) 22/5 23/5 28/5 JAN 5/8 8/5 9/32 (wireless)
20/12 120m W Liz Liz 21/12 Dov 22/12 Thames H 27/12 1923 Thames H(c) 4/1 Dss 6/1 7/1 (40m E Lands E)

FEB 7/40 9/34 20/45 MARCH 1/33 (wireless) 3/3 5/2 8/2 10/3
Baton R 29/1 NO 29/1 NO 8/2 28/2 180m SW Lands E Dov 2/3 Lo 4/3 Lo(c) 9/3 Lo 9/3

12/6 12/3 (wireless) APRIL 3/11 18/45 MAY 1/18 3/2
Bchy 10/3 11/3 45m S Lands E 18/3 100m S NO 1/4 30/4 140m SW Lands E Dov 2/5

| SHIPS NAME | NET TONNAGE | PORT OF REGISTRY | CAPTAIN |
|---|---|---|---|
| | | | J D SCOTT |
| TOWING BARGE NAVAHOE | 5772 | BELFAST | J NEWAL 3/1/1923 |
| | | | J. D. SCOTT 7/3/1923 |
| IROQUOIS (BRIT.) | | | |

YEAR
1923/24

4/2 5/3 10/2 12/4 14/7 | JUNE | 15/32 28/20 (wireless) 29/5
Thames H 2/5 Lo 4/5 Lo(c) 9/5 Lo 11/5 Liz 15/5 P Eads 2/6 27/6 250 m SW Valentia Baton R 6/6

29/6 (wireless) 30/7 | JULY | 2/13 6/11 9/14 14/8 16/4 16/19 (wireless)
28/6 200 m W of Liz 20/6 Spurn 1/9 Hull 4/7 Hull 6/7 Spurn 12/7 Bchy 13/7 14/7 30 m S of Liz

AUG | 24/33 27/17 (wireless) 28/18 (wireless) 30/2 | SEPT | 1/2 3/2 3/3
P. Eads 13/8 26/8 160 m S of Valentia 27/8 40 m W of Lands E Lo 24/8 Lo(c) 31/8 Lo 1/9 Snd 2/9

5/34 (wireless) 6/22 | NOV | Towing Barge 22/2 22/20 23/19 (wireless) | DEC | 29/35
2/9 40 m NE of N. Fore NWtg 3/9 Dov 21/11 NWtg 20/11 22/11 60 m S Lands E Sabine 18/12

JAN | 12/6 14/5 15/4 18/3 21/13 Anchor cable slipped/passed over due to fouling buoy 28/14 | FEB | 15/16 15/9 16/11 18/5
1924 | Liz 11/1 Dov 12/1 Lo 13/1 Lo 17/1 Shlds 20/1 Newc 26/1 Newc 14/2 Shlds 14/2 Flam 14/2 Spit 17/2

19/20 (wireless) FEB 20/33 (wireless) | MARCH | 6/30 10/17 see Navahoe Barge 24/19 (wireless) 26/2 31/1
18/2 Lands E 19/2 (Valentia) NY 4/3 8/3 In Sandy H. Bay 23/31 Lands E Lo 25/3 Lo (c) 29/3

APRIL | 1/4 2/4 3/20 (wireless) 30/28 30/28 (wireless) | MAY | 18/19 (wireless) 20/22 (wireless)
Lo 31/3 Dov 31/3 1/4 Lands E Baton R 28/4 18/5 (Valentia) 18/5 (Valentia) 19/5 170 m SW Lands E

21/5 22/4 23/3 27/2 28/3 29/4 30/20 (wireless) 31/18 (wireless)
Liz 20/5 Dov 21/5 Lo 22/5 Lo (c) 26/5 Lo 27/5 I W 28/5 28/5 Lands E 30/5 250 m SW of Valentia

| SHIPS NAME | NET TONNAGE | PORT OF REGISTRY | CAPTAIN |
|---|---|---|---|
| | | | J D SCOTT |
| TOWING BARGE NAVAHOE | 5772 | BELFAST | J NEWAL 16/1/1924 |
| | | | J D SCOTT 24/5/1924 |
| IROQUOIS (BRIT.) | | | |

YEAR
1924/25

JUNE 26/32 JULY 12/32 14/17 (wireless) 15/7 16/5 17/3 22/3 23/3 24/5
P. Eads 17/6 Baton R 17/6 13/7 Valentia Liz 14/7 Bchy 15/7 Lo 16/7 Lo (c) 21/7 Lo 22/7 Dss 22/7

Propeller Damage; Towing Prometheus
24/17 (wireless) AUG 21/19 22/32 22/15 27/34 SEPT 1/35 6/16 19/19 (wireless)
23/7 Lands E NO 19/8 Baton R 17/8 NO 20/8 NO 25/8 NO 30/8 NY 4/9 18/9 (Valentia)

Collision in R. Thames
20/20 (wireless) 22/3 26/3 29/2 29/4 30/6 30/21 (wireless) OCT 3/4 16/18 25/4
19/9 Lands E Dss 21/9 Lo 25/9 Lo (c) 27/9 Lo 28/9 Bchy 28/9 29/9 (Lands E) Lo 2/10 Lo 15/10

Towing Navahoe; see Navahoe; Grounded in River
18/33 24/36 NOV 15/5 17/3 20/2 21/2 22/6 24/24 (wireless) DEC 18/17 got off 24/41
NO 16/10 N 22/10 Liz 14/11 Lo 16/11 Lo (c) 19/11 Lo 20/11 IW 21/11 21/11 (Lands E) NO 16/12 NO 20/12

JAN 12/22 (wireless) 14/5 17/3 21/2 23/5 24/7 26/7 FEB 19/34 23/41
1925 11/1 (Lands E) Dov 13/1 Lo 16/1 Lo (c) 20/1 Lo 22/1 IW 23/1 Liz 24/1 Baton R 16/2 NO 20/2

MARCH 16/21 (wireless) 17/18 (wireless) 18/4 19/3 23/2 24/6 25/35 (wireless) 25/7 26/6
14/3 (Valentia) 16/3 (Lands E) Dss 17/3 Lo 18/3 Lo (c) 21/3 Lo 23/3 24/3 (Niton) Liz 25/3 Tor B 24/3

27/19 (wireless) 28/21 (wireless) APRIL 13/19 15/33 27/19 (wireless) 28/20 (wireless) 29/4
25/3 (Lands E) 26/3 (Valentia) NY 9/4 NY 12/4 25/4 (Valentia) 26/4 (Lands E) Bchy 28/4

30/4 MAY 5/6 6/4 8/12 28/9 29/6 30/6 JUNE 2/8
Lo 29/4 Lo 4/5 Snd 4/5 Shlds 7/5 Shlds 26/5 Bchy 28/5 IW 28/5 Pwle 30/5

| SHIPS NAME | NET TONNAGE | PORT OF REGISTRY | CAPTAIN |
|---|---|---|---|
| | | | J. D. SCOTT |
| TOWING BARGE NAVAHOE | 5772 | BELFAST | W PRITCHARD 26/9/1924 |
| IROQUOIS (BRIT.) | | | |

YEAR
1925/26

2/22 (wireless) 22/41 27/3 | JULY | 8/31 14/19 (wireless) 15/42 (wireless) (see Navahoe) 17/5 18/4 21/3
30/5 (Lands E) NO 20/6 NO 25/6 P. Eads 25/6 27/6 NY 14/7 (Lands E) Dov 16/7 Lo 17/7 Lo(c) 20/7

22/3 23/4 24/29 (wireless) 27/28 (wireless) | AUG | Grounded 19/29 | SEPT | 5/23 (wireless) Towing Navahoe 7/24 (wireless)
Lo 21/7 IW 22/7 23/7 (Lands E) 24/7 310m SW of Valentia NO 16/8 3/9 (Valentia) 6/9 (Niton)

8/5 10/2 10/2 11/6 Towing Navahoe 22/6 (wireless) 14/8 | OCT | 5/37 9/29 Heavy weather damage 27/19 (wireless)
Lo 7/9 Lo(c) Lo 10/9 Bchy 11/9 11/9 (Niton) Liz 11/9 NO 2/10 NO 7/10 26/10 (Valentia)

Towing Navahoe 28/41 (wireless) 29/5 30/4 | NOV | 2/2 3/6 4/5 4/39 (wireless) 6/34 (wireless) 6/6
26/10 (Valentia) IW 28/10 Lo 29/10 Lo(c) 31/10 Lo 2/11 Bchy 3/11 3/11 (Niton) 5/11 (Lands E) Bxm 3/11

6/6 7/23 (wireless) 25/32 | DEC | 2/46 14/16 (wireless) 15/47 16/6 17/5 19/14
Bxm 4/11 5/11 (Valentia) NY 23/11 NY 29/11 12/12 (Valentia) Turks I 4/12 Liz 15/12 Bchy 16/12 Hull 18/12

22/19 22/5 23/5 24/4 28/6 28/37 (wireless) 29/5 | JAN | FEB | 6/3
Hull 19/12 Dss 21/12 Spit 22/12 Son 22/12 Spit 22/6 27/12 (Lands E) Liz 27/12 | 1926 | NO 4/2

23/8 24/9 25/5 27/4 | MARCH | 4/6 5/3 Towing 5/5 6/15 (wireless)
Liz 22/2 Bchy 23/2 Thames H 24/2 Thames H (c) 26/2 IW 3/3 Thames 2/3 Liz 4/3 4/3 (Lands E)

30/46 | APRIL | 7/42 17/36 26/15 (wireless) 27/6 28/5 29/4 30/5
NO 28/3 NO 4/4 P. Eads 4/4 24/4 200m SW Valentia Pule 26/4 Dov 27/4 Thames H 28/4 Thames H 29/4

| SHIPS NAME | NET TONNAGE | PORT OF REGISTRY | CAPTAIN |
|---|---|---|---|
| | | | W PRITCHARD |
| TOWING BARGE NAVAHOE | 5772 | BELFAST | |
| IROQUOIS (BRIT.) | | | |

YEAR 1926/27

MAY 4/4 6/4 7/3 8/3 29/30 JUNE 3/29 17/19 22/12 (wireless) 23/33 (wireless — see Navahoe)
ThamesH(c) 3/5 Snd 5/5 IW 6/5 Pirle 6/5 NO 27/5 NO 1/6 KeyW 30/6 21/6 (Valentia) 22/6 (Lands E)

24/16 (wireless) 24/6 25/6 29/6 29/6 JULY 1/8 6/17 9/7 9/15 (wireless)
23/6 (Niton) Pirle 23/6 Lo 24/6 Lo 28/6 Snd 28/6 Shlds 30/6 Shlds 5/8 Spit 8/8 8/8 15m W of Niton

10/7 AUG 10/16 (wireless) SEPT 2/23 6/12 7/11 8/21 30/27 (wireless)
Collision with Navahoe ? Proc 2/9 will Proc 6/9 outside pass 6/32
IW 8/8 8/8 (Lands E) NO 31/8 NO 4/9 NO 4/9 (NY) 4/9 (Lo) 7/9 29/9 (Lands E)

OCT 1/7 2/6 4/6 5/7 8/16 for Bm 25/18 25/18 26/31 (wireless) 27/10
Liz 30/9 Bchy 1/10 Snd 2/10 ThamesH 2/10 Shlds 7/10 Shlds 23/10 Flam 23/10 25/10 (Niton) IW 25/10

28/4 28/4 28/5 28/15 (wireless) NOV 15/36 16/36 29/18 (wireless) 30/16 (wireless)
TorB 26/10 TorB 26/10 Liz 27/10 27/10 (Lands E) NY 12/11 NY 14/11 28/11 (Lands E) 29/11 (Niton)

DEC 1/3 1/3 2/4 4/3 6/5 7/5 7/18 (wireless) Towing Navahoe 8/6 29/35 JAN 5/28
Dov 30/11 Snd 30/11 Lo 1/12 Lo(c) 3/12 Lo 5/12 Snd 5/12 6/12 (Niton) Liz 6/12 NO 26/12 1927 NO 2/1

24/15 (wireless) 25/3 28/2 31/4 31/17 (wireless) FEB 1/4 2/33 (wireless) 2/39 23/33 MARCH
23/1 (Niton) Lo 24/1 Lo(c) 27/1 Lo 29/1 30/11 (Niton) Liz 31/15 31/1 (Lands E) NY 19/2 NY 21/2

8/15 (wireless) 9/5 10/4 11/4 12/2 15/5 19/6 21/6 21/15 (wireless)
6/3 300m SW Valentia Liz 8/3 Bchy 9/3 Lo 10/3 Lo(c) 11/3 Lo 14/3 Snd 18/3 Dss 18/3 19/3 50m SE Lands E

| SHIPS NAME | NET TONNAGE | PORT OF REGISTRY | CAPTAIN |
|---|---|---|---|
| | | | W PRITCHARD |
| TOWING BARGE NAVAHOE | 5772 | BELFAST | T N HUGO 24/6/1927 |

IROQUOIS (BRIT.)

YEAR
1927/28

APRIL 9/32 12/36 23/15 (wireless) 25/7 25/14 (wireless) 26/4 27/2 30/4
NY 7/4 NY 9/4 21/4 360m SW Valentia Pwle 24/4 24/4 (Niton) Lo 25/4 Lo(c) 26/4 Lo 29/4

MAY 2/7 26/27 30/35 JUNE 21/6 22/4 23/3 23/3 25/3 27/4 27/5
Pwle 30/4 Houst 23/5 Houst 26/5 Pwle 20/6 Dov 21/6 Lo 22/6 Thames H 21/6 Lo(c) 24/6 Lo 25/6 Dss 26/6

Towing 28/6 JULY 20/30 25/35 AUG 11/6 12/5 15/2 16/5 17/5 SEPT 8/29 13/23
IW 26/6 NO 18/9 NO 23/7 Pwle 10/8 Lo 11/8 Lo(c) 13/8 Lo 15/8 IW 16/8 NO 6/9 NO 12/9

28/19 OCT 1/7 3/3 4/3 5/3 7/8 24/21 24/21 NOV 14/35
P. Eads 11/9 Pwle 30/9 Lo 2/10 Lo(c) 3/10 Lo 4/10 Shlds 6/10 Shlds 22/10 Flam 22/10 NY 12/11

17/29 DEC 1/4 2/4 3/4 5/2 6/5 7/5 29/36 JAN 7/28
NY 15/11 Pwle 30/11 Dov 1/12 Lo 2/12 Lo(c) 3/12 Lo 5/12 Bchy 6/12 NY 29/12 1928 Houst 4/1

12/27 30/5 31/4 FEB 2/2 3/3 3/3 4/5 6/5 7/7 for Repairs 22/26
Houst 7/1 Liz 29/1 Lo 30/1 Lo(c) 1/2 Lo 2/2 Snd 2/2 IW 3/2 Pwle 3/2 Qtns 5/2 Qtn 23/2

22/26 23/24 APRIL 13/5 14/5 17/3 18/3 18/3 19/3 MAY 14/33
Houst 19/3 Houst 20/3 IW 12/4 Lo 13/4 Lo(c) 16/4 Lo 17/4 Dov 17/14 Dss 17/4 Houst 10/5

17/27 JUNE 6/6 7/3 8/3 9/3 9/5 11/2 12/6 13/6 JULY
Houst 14/5 Liz 5/6 Dss 6/6 Lo 7/6 Lo(c) 8/6 Thames H 8/6 Lo 10/6 Bchy 11/6 Pwle 12/6 Houst 4/7

| SHIPS NAME | NET TONNAGE | PORT OF REGISTRY | CAPTAIN |
|---|---|---|---|
| | | | W PRITCHARD |
| TOWING BARGE NAVAHOE | 5772 | BELFAST | T N HUGO 24/6/1927 |
| | | | W PRITCHARD 13/8/1927 |
| IROQUOIS (BRIT.) | | | |

YEAR
1928|29|30

26/6 27/5 28/4 30/1 31/5 AUG 1/6 2/1 30/26 SEPT 15/5 17/3
Liz 25/7 Bchy 26/4 Lo 27/7 Lo(c) 28/7 Lo 30/7 1W 31/7 Pwle 31/7 NO 28/8 Liz 14/9 Lo 6/9

18/4 21/5 21/5 22/9 22/9 OCT 10/7 12/5 15/5 NOV 7/36 9/23
Lo(c) 17/9 Lo 20/9 Snd 20/9 Flam 21/9 Shlds 21/9 Shlds 9/10 1W 11/10 Pwle 12/10 Galv 3/11 Howst 6/11

DEC 1/5 3/3 4/3 5/3 6/5 7/5 7/5 8/6 JAN 2/28 4/24 23/4
Pwle 30/11 Lo 1/12 Lo(c) 3/12 Lo 4/12 1W 5/1 TorB 5/12 Pwle 5/12 Liz 6/12 1929 Howst 29/12 Howst 31/12 Liz 22/1

24/4 26/3 26/4 26/4 29/6 MARCH 1/28 19/4 20/4 22/3
Dov 23/1 Lo(c) 25/1 ThamesH 25/1 ThamesH 25/1 Pwle 28/1 NO 26/2 Bchy 18/3 Dov 18/3 ThamesH 20/3

22/3 26/5 APRIL 1/10 20/32 26/30 MAY 10/2 15/5 16/4 17/2
ThamesH(c) 25/3 ThamesH 25/3 Dss 28/3 NO 18/4 NO 24/4 P. Eads 24/4 Bchy 14/5 Lo 15/5 Lo(c) 16/5

21/4 21/5 JUNE 17/33 19/33 JULY 8/7 9/6 10/4 11/2 13/6 AUG
Lo 17/5 Pwle 19/5 Howst 13/6 Galv 15/6 Liz 7/7 Dov 8/7 ThamesH 9/7 Thames (c) 10/7 Bchy 12/7

8/31 29/4 30/3 SEPT 3/5 3/6 4/4 5/4 5/4 27/32 Towing 30/36 OCT 21/5 22/4
Howst 5/8 Lo 28/8 Lo(c) 29/8 Lo 2/9 Snd 2/9 1W 3/9 Bxm 3/9 Bxm 3/9 Howst 25/9 Howst 26/9 Dov 2/10 Lo 21/10

23/2 25/3 28/19 NOV 16/7 18/5 19/5 DEC 10/37 23/35 JAN 11/7 13/3
Lo(c) 22/10 Lo 24/10 Mbro 26/10 Mbro 14/11 1W 16/11 Pwle 18/11 NO 14/12 NO 19/12 1930 Pwle 10/1 Lo 12/1

| SHIPS NAME | NET TONNAGE | PORT OF REGISTRY | CAPTAIN |
|---|---|---|---|
| | | | W PRITCHARD |
| TOWING BARGE NAVAHOE | 5772 | BELFAST | W. Barrows 10/7/29 |
| | | | W. PRITCHARD 28/8/29 |
| IROQUOIS (BRIT.) | | | |

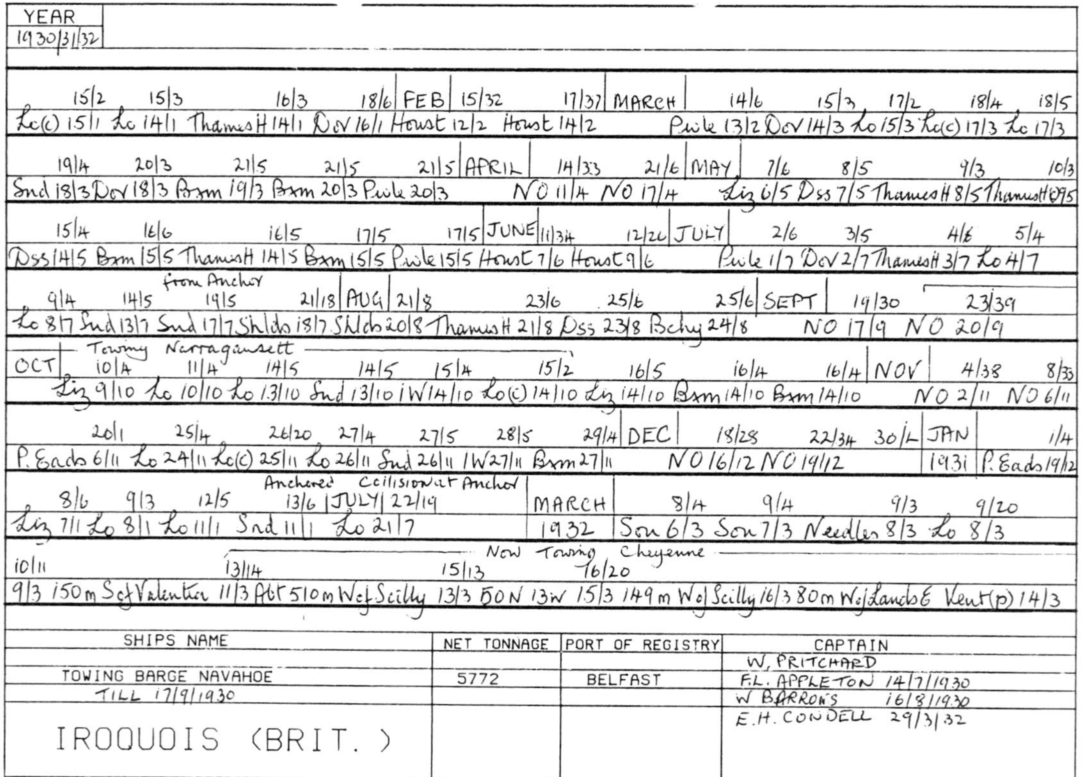

YEAR
1930/31/32

15/2 15/3 16/3 18/6 FEB 15/32 17/37 MARCH 14/6 15/3 17/2 18/4 18/5
Lo(c) 15/1 Lo 14/1 Thames H 14/1 Dov 16/1 Houst 12/2 Houst 14/2 Pwle 13/2 Dov 14/3 Lo 15/3 Lo(c) 17/3 Lo 17/3

19/4 20/3 21/5 21/5 21/5 APRIL 14/33 21/6 MAY 7/6 8/5 9/3 10/3
Snd 18/3 Dov 18/3 Bxm 19/3 Bxm 20/3 Pwle 20/3 NO 11/4 NO 17/4 Liz 6/5 Dss 7/5 Thames H 8/5 Thames H 9/5

15/4 16/6 16/5 17/5 17/5 JUNE 11/34 12/26 JULY 2/6 3/5 4/6 5/4
Dss 14/5 Bxm 15/5 Thames H 14/5 Bxm 15/5 Pwle 15/5 Houst 7/6 Houst 9/6 Pwle 1/7 Dov 2/7 Thames H 3/7 Lo 4/7

from Anchor
9/4 14/5 19/5 21/18 AUG 21/8 23/6 25/6 25/6 SEPT 19/30 23/39
Lo 8/7 Snd 13/7 Snd 17/7 Shlds 18/7 Shlds 20/8 Thames H 21/8 Dss 23/8 Bchy 24/8 NO 17/9 NO 20/9

Towing Narragansett
OCT 10/4 11/4 14/5 14/5 15/4 15/2 16/5 16/4 16/4 NOV 4/38 8/33
Liz 9/10 Lo 10/10 Lo 13/10 Snd 13/10 IW 14/10 Lo(c) 14/10 Liz 14/10 Bxm 14/10 Bxm 14/10 NO 2/11 NO 6/11

20/1 25/4 26/20 27/4 27/5 28/5 29/4 DEC 18/28 22/34 30/L JAN 1/4
P. Eads 6/11 Lo 24/11 Lo(c) 25/11 Lo 26/11 Snd 26/11 IW 27/11 Bxm 27/11 NO 16/12 NO 19/12 1931 P. Eads 19/12

Anchored Collision at Anchor
8/6 9/3 12/5 13/6 JULY 22/19 MARCH 8/4 9/4 9/3 9/20
Liz 7/1 Lo 8/1 Lo 11/1 Snd 11/1 Lo 21/7 1932 Son 6/3 Son 7/3 Needles 8/3 Lo 8/3

Now Towing Cheyenne
10/11 13/14 15/13 16/20
9/3 150m S of Valentia 11/3 Abt 510m W of Scilly 13/3 50N 13W 15/3 149m W of Scilly 16/3 80m W of Lands E Kent(p) 14/3

| SHIPS NAME | NET TONNAGE | PORT OF REGISTRY | CAPTAIN |
|---|---|---|---|
| TOWING BARGE NAVAHOE TILL 17/9/1930 | 5772 | BELFAST | W. PRITCHARD<br>F.L. APPLETON 14/7/1930<br>W BARROWS 16/8/1930<br>E.H. CONDELL 29/3/32 |
| IROQUOIS (BRIT.) | | | |

YEAR
1932 – 35

19/4 31/4 APRIL 1/4 | DEC | DRAGGED ANCHOR 24/16 27/14 Removed 24/12 29/16 | DEC | 21/5 21/5
Thames H 18/3 B chy 20/3 Fal 31/3 Fal 23/12 23/12 Fal 25/12 | 1933 | Fal 20/12 Liz 20/12

JAN | 12/35 15/40 | FEB | 1/4 3/7 3/7 3/7 5/4 6/9 27/44 | MARCH | 6/41
1934 | NO 10/1 NO 13/1 Liv 30/1 Stanlow 31/1 Stanlow 1/2 Esthm 1/2 Glas 2/2 Glas 4/2 NO 25/2 NO 3/3

23/4 24/4 26/2 26/6 26/6 27/6 | MAY | 3/7 9/21 11/28 23/31 30/23
Pwle 22/3 Lo 23/3 Lo(c) 24/3 Lo 25/3 Snd 25/3 Dss 25/3 Gib(p) 2/5 Alg 3/5 Alg 5/5 Trip(Syria) 11/5 Trip(Syria) 19/5

31/25 31/26 31/26 | JUNE | 4/35 4/34 5/31 11/31 13/15 14/4 15/5 16/6 16/6 16/4
Istan 26/5 Istan 26/5 Haifa 20/5 Cstza 27/5 Istan 31/5 Cstza 31/5 Gib(p) 8/6 Usht 12/6 Dov 13/6 Lo 13/6 Lo 15/6 Snd 15/6 Dov 15/6

18/6 19/9 21/8 21/8 22/8 29/8 × 30/7 | NOV | 17/33 20/46 | DEC | 11/5 12/3 12/2 13/6
Pwle 16/6 Mchr 18/6 Mchr 19/6 Esthm 20/6 Belf 21/6 Belf 27/10 NO 15/11 NO 18/11 Liz 10/22 Lo 11/12 Lo(c) 11/12 Lo 12/12

13/6 14/4 15/6 17/8 18/8 19/5 19/5 24/8 24/6 27/5 27/6 | JAN | 1/12
Snd 12/12 IW 13/12 Liz 13/12 Mchr 15/12 Mchr 17/12 Esthm 17/12 Liv 18/12 Liv 22/12 Liz 23/12 Dss 26/12 Sou 25/12 | 1935 | Nybg 29/12

3/9 4/6 26/33 | FEB | 4/6 15/7 16/7 16/2 16/2 18/8 18/7 19/7 20/7
Nybg 31/12 Dunnet 3/1 NO 24/1 NO 26/1 Barry I 14/2 Avon 14/2 Avon 15/2 Barry I 15/2 Liv 16/2 Esthm 16/2 Mchr 17/2 Mchr 19/2

21/6 23/3 25/1 25/3 25/3 24/5 | MARCH | 4/7 5/5 12/12 12/12 12/8 | APRIL | 2/42
Esthm 19/2 Lo 22/2 Lo(c) 23/2 Lo 24/2 Dov 24/2 Sou 24/2 Fawley 3/3 Dss 3/3 Nybg 7/3 Nybg 8/3 Dunnet 10/3 NO 31/3

| SHIPS NAME | NET TONNAGE | PORT OF REGISTRY | CAPTAIN |
| --- | --- | --- | --- |
| | | | EH CONDELL 29/3/32 |
| | 5772 | BELFAST | W BARRONS 18/12/33 |
| IROQUOIS (BRIT.) | | | |

YEAR
1935/36

8/36 18/20 26/3 27/2 27/4 27/5 29/4 30/8 MAY 1/6 2/4 3/6 4/6
NO 4/4 P Eads 5/4 Lo 25/4 Lo(c) 26/4 Lo 26/4 Dov 26/4 Avon 28/4 Barry I 29/4 Esthm 30/4 Mchr 1/5 Mchr 2/5 Esthm 2/5

27/33 JUNE 12/7 13/3 15/4 15/6 17/7 17/7 18/8 19/6 21/6 21/6 24/7(w) 25/4
NO 2A/5 Bchy 11/6 Lo 12/6 Lo 13/6 Dov 14/6 Avon 15/6 Avon 16/6 Esthm 17/6 Mchr 17/6 Mchr 19/6 Esthm 20/6 Liz 23/6 Liz 24/6

"D.L. Harper"
26/6 JULY 6/6 6/5 9/16 11/4 11/19 30/39 AUG 3/34 20/6 21/2 21/4 22/4 23/5
Fal 24/6 Fal 4/7 Dss 5/7 Ham 7/7 Ham 9/7 Ham 8/7 NO 28/4 NO 28/4 Lo 19/8 Lo(c) 20/8 Lo 20/8 Pwle 21/8 Liz 21/8

24/8 26/8 27/8 28/5 SEPT 17/42 20/36 OCT 7/7 8/4 9/5 9/6 10/4 11/5
Esthm 23/8 Mchr 2A/8 Mchr 26/8 Esthm 27/8 NO 14/9 NO 17/9 Pwle 6/10 Lo 7/10 Lo 8/10 Dov 8/10 IW 9/10 Barry I 10/10

Put in with Engine trouble 2/19 · Sailed 13/26 · mishap at berth 25/21
12/5 12/5 12/6 15/7 16/6 17/6 NOV 1/6
Avon 10/10 Avon 11/10 Barry I 11/10 Mchr 14/10 Esthm 14/10 Belf 15/10 Belf 30/10 Qtn 1/11 12/11 Lo 23/11

DEC 3/42 6/32 23/5 24/5 24/6 27/8 30/7 30/7 JAN 24/32 FEB 3/6
NO 30/11 NO 3/12 Avon 22/12 Avon 22/12 Barry I 22/12 Mchr 26/12 Mchr 28/12 Esthm 29/12 1936 NO 21/1 NO 2A/1

14/6 14/6 17/2 17/4 18/5 19/5 19/6 20/5 21/5 21/5 22/8 24/4 24/4
Liz 12/2 Lo 14/2 Lo(c) 14/2 Lo 15/2 Dov 17/2 Bchy 17/2 Pwle 18/2 Barry I 19/2 Avon 19/2 Avon 20/2 Esthm 21/2 Mchr 22/2 Mchr 23/2

25/6 27/6 APRIL 4/8 6/6 7/6 7/5 8/5 14/34 14/35 15/7 17/11
Esthm 24/2 Belf 25/2 Belf 2/4 Needles 4/4 Dov 6/4 Spit 6/4 Dss 6/4 C/bn 9/4 Eb 11/4 Dunnet 13/4 C/bn 11/4

| SHIPS NAME | NET TONNAGE | PORT OF REGISTRY | CAPTAIN |
| --- | --- | --- | --- |
| | | | W. BARRONS |
| | 5772 | BELFAST | J.M JACKSON 27/12/1935 |
| | | | W BARRONS 21/3/1936 |
| IROQUOIS (BRIT.) | | | |

YEAR
1936/37

MAY 5/45 8/24 16/37 24/4 26/5 26/4 27/5 27/5 27/5 28/4 29/7 30/7
NO 3/5 NO 5/5 Baton R 4/5 Dov 24/5 Lo 24/5 Lo(c) 25/5 Lo 26/5 Snd 26/5 Dov 26/5 Liz 27/5 Liv 28/5 Mchr 29/5

JUNE 2/21 2/20 2/22 2/22 2/22 4/4 5/6 6/5 6/6 6/6 9/15 11/4
Mchr 30/5 Esthm 30/5 Glas 31/5 Glas 1/6 Tail of B 1/6 Pwle 3/6 Needles 3/6 Dss 4/6 Sou 3/6 Sou 4/6 Nybg 8/6 Nybg 8/6

13/9 JULY 3/30 15/9 18/4 23/5 23/5 23/6 24/8 24/8 25/8 27/9
Dunnet 12/1 NO 1/7 NO 4/7 Baton R 3/7 Avon 21/7 Avon 22/7 Barry I 22/7 Liv 23/7 Esthm 23/7 Mchr 24/7 Mchr 25/7

27/9 AUG 15/32 18/45 18/45 24/4 SEPT 4/5 5/3 7/11 7/2 7/4 8/5
Esthm 26/7 NO 13/8 Baton R 14/8 NO 16/8 P. Eads 17/8 Dss 3/9 Lo 3/9 Spurn 6/9 Lo(c) 5/9 Lo 5/9 Hull 6/9

9/7 9/7 21/6 OCT 22/6 22/7 23/8 24/7 26/9 26/10 27/7
Hull 7/9 Spurn 8/9 Avon 20/10 Avon 20/10 Barry I 20/10 Esthm 22/10 Mchr 22/10 Esthm 25/10 Mchr 24/10 Glas 26/10

27/7 29/8 29/7 NOV 2/9 Regrounding in Canal 4/26 20/34 23/43 DEC 11/7
Glas 26/10 Hunglass 27/10 Belf 28/10 Belf 30/10 (Lo) 3/11 NO 18/11 NO 21/11 Barry I 10/12

12/7 12/7 14/9 15/8 15/8 15/8 17/6 19/5 19/4 21/4
Avon 10/12 Avon 11/12 Esthm 12/12 Irlam 13/12 Mchr 13/12 Mchr 14/12 Esthm 15/12 Liz 17/12 Dss 18/12 Lo 19/12 Lo 20/12

21/5 22/4 22/8 23/4 23/4 23/4 JAN 11/40 23/38 FEB 3/6
Snd 20/12 Lo(c) 19/12 Pwle 21/12 Fal 21/12 Fal 21/12 Liz 21/12 1937 NO 9/1 Baton R 11/1 Barry I 2/2

| SHIPS NAME | NET TONNAGE | PORT OF REGISTRY | CAPTAIN |
|---|---|---|---|
| | | | W BARRONS |
| | 5772 | BELFAST | |
| IROQUOIS (BRIT.) | | | |

YEAR
1937/38

4/5 5/5 5/5 6/7 8/8 8/8 10/4 11/5 12/4 12/4 13/6
Avon 2/2 Avon 3/2 Barry 9 4/2 Esthm 5/2 Esthm 7/2 Mckr 6/2 Needles 9/2 Son 9/2 Spit 11/2 Fawley 11/2 Son 11/2

13/5 17/10 18/10 19/10 20/12 22/14 23/14 24/7 MARCH 22/41 25/36
Dss 11/2 Skaw 14/2 Els 17/2 Gdy 16/2 Cpn 17/2 Nybg 18/2 Nybg 19/2 Dunmet 22/2 NO 19/3 NO 22/3

APRIL 13/8 13/8 14/6 15/5 16/6 16/6 17/8 19/9 19/8 21/7 MAY 8/7
Barry 9 12/4 Avon 12/4 Avon 13/4 Barry 9 13/4 Liv 15/4 Liv 10/4 Mckr 16/4 Mckr 16/4 Esthm 18/4 Bel 19/4 Bel 6/5

10/6 13/6 13/7 15/15 18/35 20/12 20/13 JUNE 12/36 14/40 29/6 29/6
Needles 8/5 Dss 12/5 Son 11/5 Bsble 14/5 Nybg 15/5 Nybg 16/5 Skaw 17/5 Baton R 8/6 NO 10/6 Avon 27/6 Avon 28/6

29/6 30/6 JULY 1/7 3/7 3/7 AUG 4/53 9/42 21/7 23/6 23/7
Barry 9 28/6 Liv 29/6 Mckr 30/6 Mckr 1/7 Esthm 2/7 Baton R 21/7 NO 6/8 Avon 20/8 Avon 21/8 Barry 9 21/8

24/8 25/6 25/5 27/8 27/7 30/5 OCT 1/4 11/17 11/14 13/10 13/10
Liv 23/8 Liv 24/8 Mckr 24/8 Mckr 26/8 Esthm 26/8 Liz 29/8 Dss 30/9 Els 10/10 Oxelo 8/10 Gbg 11/10 Oxelo 9/10

14/10 15/4 16/3 NOV 4/40 9/45 20/20 29/2 30/4 DEC 1/4 2/9
Gbg 11/10 Dss 14/10 Bcky 14/10 NO 2/11 Baton R 5/11 P. Eads 6/11 Lo 28/11 Lo(c) 28/11 Lo 29/4 Spurn 30/11

3/9 4/10 4/10 6/5 20/56 JAN 4/38 7/11 20/5 21/5 21/5
Hull 2/12 Hull 3/12 Spurn 3/12 Pwle 4/12 NO 24/12 1938 Baton R 26/12 NO 28/12 Avon 18/1 Avon 19/1 Barry 9 19/1

| SHIPS NAME | NET TONNAGE | PORT OF REGISTRY | CAPTAIN |
|---|---|---|---|
| | | | W. BARRONS |
| | 5772 | BELFAST | C. CRUIKSHANK 30/6/37 |
| | | | W BARRONS 24/8/37 |
| IROQUOIS (BRIT.) | | | |

YEAR
1938/39

22/7 24/8 25/7 25/6 26/7 (Anchor) 28/6 29/7 MARCH 1/43 4/10 16/3
Esthm 21/1 Runc 21/1 Mchr 23/1 Esthm 24/1 Liv 24/1 R. Mersey 27/1 Liv 28/1 Baton R 20/2 NO 21/2 ~~Lo~~ NO 15/3

18/3 19/7 21/10 21/10 21/9 APRIL 4/10 6/4 7/5 27/29 30/32 30/32
Lo 17/3 Spurn 18/3 Hull 18/3 Spurn 19/3 Shlds 20/3 Shlds 3/4 Dss 5/4 Liz 6/4 NO 25/4 Baton R. 27/4 NO 28/4

MAY 18/4 19/2 21/4 21/5 23/12 23/12 24/10 24/7 JUNE 16/36 22/4 JULY 4/9
Lo 17/5 Lo (c) 18/5 Lo 19/5 Snd 19/5 Hull 20/5 Spurn 22/5 Hull 22/5 Pwle 23/5 NO 14/6 Baton R 13/6 Avon 2/7

re mishap in Canal 4/7
4/9 5/9 6/6 7/6 7/29 8/6 8/6 11/8 29/28 AUG 4/34 13/6 19/5
Avon 3/7 Esthm 4/7 Mchr 5/7 Mchr 6/7 (Mchr) 6/7 Esthm 7/7 Liv 7/7 Liv 9/7 NO 27/7 NO 1/8 P. Eads 1/8 Avon 17/8

20/6 20/6 22/9 22/9 22/9 23/8 SEPT 12/39 16/34 30/4 OCT 4/5 5/2
Avon 18/8 Barry 19/8 Liv 20/8 Liv 20/8 Glas 21/8 Glas 22/8 NO 10/9 NO 14/9 P. Eads 15/9 Lo 3/10 Lo (c) 4/10

6/4 6/8 10/11 10/11 11/6 11/10 12/5 NOV 1/46 4/37 25/3 25/2 26/5
Lo 4/10 Spurn 5/10 Hull 8/10 Spurn 9/10 Dss 10/10 Hull 9/10 Pwle 11/10 NO 29/10 NO 2/11 Lo 24/11 Lo (c) 24/11 Lo 25/11

28/11 29/9 29/9 29/5 30/4 DEC Been aground outside 24/20 S. Pass JAN 3/A 3/F 13/4
Spurn 27/11 Hull 26/11 Hull 27/11 Dss 28/11 IW 28/11 (NO) 22/12 1939 NO 22/12 Baton R 21/12 Dss 12/1

14/9 16/9 16/9 18/2 18/4 18/5 19/4 20/4 20/4 21/5 24/14 26/11 27/13 30/10
Spurn 13/1 Hull 14/1 Lo 14/1 Lo (c) 16/1 Lo 17/1 Dss 17/1 Spit 18/1 Son 18/1 Son 19/1 Dss 19/1 Bsbte 21/1 Nybg 23/1 Nybg 25/1 Mbro 27/1

| SHIPS NAME | NET TONNAGE | PORT OF REGISTRY | CAPTAIN |
|---|---|---|---|
| | 5772 | BELFAST | W BARRONS |
| IROQUOIS (BRIT.) | | | |

YEAR 1939/40

FEB 12/10 13/6 14/6 MARCH 8/28 29/6 30/5 30/5 31/5 APRIL 1/7 1/8
Mbro 10/2 Son 12/2 Needles 12/2 Galv 6/3 Avon 27/3 Avon 29/3 Barry 29/3 Esthm 20/3 Mchr 30/3 Mchr 31/3

In Collision 31/3
3/6 6/30 29/37 MAY 18/6 19/6 19/7 20/8 22/8 23/7 25/7 26/8
Esthm 1/4 (Mchr) 5/4 Baton R 26/4 Avon 17/5 Avon 18/5 Barry 18/5 Liv 19/5 Liv 21/5 Glas 22/5 Glas 23/5 Tail of B 23/5

JUNE 17/37 20/47 JULY 5/6 7/7 7/6 12/7 12/7 14/7 15/8 AUG 4/35
NO 14/6 Baton R 13/6 Glas 4/7 Glas 5/7 Liv 6/7 Liv 10/7 Mchr 11/7 Mchr 13/7 Esthm 14/7 NO 2/8

at Anchor
15/19 18/2 24/5 26/6 26/6 28/7 29/6 30/6 SEPT 21/19 25/28 30/22
Baton R 4/8 NO 7/8 Avon 23/8 Avon 25/8 Barry 25/8 Liv 26/8 R. Mersey 28/8 Liv 28/8 NO 19/9 21/9 NY 27/9

Anchored
Grounded in Humber 2/11
OCT 7/21 30/6 NOV 2/5 4/11 6/14 6/14 8/9 9/25 DEC 27/9
NY 4/10 Downs 28/10 Snd 1/11 Spurn 2/11 Hull 3/11 4/11 S.Shlds 7/11 (Hull) 6/11 Tyne 25/12

JAN 15/16 18/5 19/4 FEB 10/23 12/29 23/25 23/25 MARCH 12/11 14/8 15/7
1940 Skles 14/1 Downs 16/1 H. Helens 18/1 Aruba 8/2 9/2 Hal 21/2 26/2 Liv 11/3 Esthm 13/3 Stanlow 14/3

16/7 18/12 18/11 19/10 21/9 23/14 26/18 28/29 APRIL 16/2 18/9 MAY 14/27 14/27
15/3 Mchr 15/3 Barton 16/3 Mchr 18/3 Esthm 19/3 Green 21/3 Glas 21/3 Glas 27/3 Glas 15/4 Green 15/4 Aruba 7/5 9/5

17/21 JUNE 3/8 8/4 11/7 11/7 28/21 JULY 1/23 6/22 23/9 26/10
Berm 15/5 Avon 1/6 Barry 6/6 Milfd Hvn 7/6 8/6 Aruba 26/6 28/6 Berm 3/7 Dunnet 22/7 Meth Rds 23-24/7

| SHIPS NAME | NET TONNAGE | PORT OF REGISTRY | CAPTAIN |
|---|---|---|---|
| | | | W BARRONS |
| | 5772 | BELFAST | M B. ROBERTS 22/5/39 |
| | | | J M JACKSON 13/12/39 |
| IROQUOIS (BRIT.) | | | |

YEAR
1940/41

27/11 27/4 27/4 SEPT 4/1 18/3 18/19 Refloated after grounding Lemons Bank 19/11 20/10 21/11
24/25/7 Flam 25/7 Sud 26/7 Lo 27/7 Lo(c) 13/9 14/9 Lo 17/9 off Haisboro' Flam 17/9 Abbs 18/9 Meth Rds 18/9

Arrived 27/20 OCT 4/8 Anchored 5/10 7/11 28/24 30/15 NOV 11/26 11/26
Methil 26/9 Meth 2/10 Meth Rds 3/10 Dunnet 5/10 Aruba 25/10 28/10 Berm 1/11 8/11

27/8 Anchored 9/7 DEC 2/8 Anchored 3/6 4/5 5/6 10/5 re collision 7/12 12/25 13/2 21/25
Belf 25/11 Belf Lough 26/11 30/11 Liv Bar 1/12 Esthm 2/12 Stanlow 3/12 Esthm 7/12 Liv 10/12 Liv 10/12 17/12

30/6 JAN 15/5 16/5 FEB 10/25 12/19 22/20 25/21 MARCH 4/21
Liv 27/12 1941 Liv 13/1 R. Mersey 14/1 Baytown 8/2 10/2 Berm 19/2 Berm 21/2 Hal 1/3

Put back engine repairs 4/23 Required Degaussing 15/23 renewed 20/23 Left Hal 17/3 20/25 APRIL 5/10 7/10 7/11 8/9
(Lo) 2/3 13/3 Hal 14/3 (Lo) 18/3 R. Clyde 3/4 Green 4/4 Bowling 5/4 R. Clyde 5-6/4

10/9 10/9 Anchored 11/9 15/7 MAY 12/26 12/26 19/29 JUNE 6 24 24
Glas 6/4 Bowling 8/4 Clyde 8/4 13/4 Aruba 6/5 9/5 Berm 16/5 30/5 Bowling 20/6 Glas 22/6

25 JULY 2 24 28 AUG 5 8 22 23 25 25
Tail of B 23/6 1/7 Aruba 22/7 Aruba 24/7 Hal 3/8 5/8 Clyde 21/8 20-21/8 Tail of B 22/8 24/8

25 25 26 29 SEPT 18 OCT 16 21 25 NOV 11 12
Glas 22/8 24/8 R. Clyde 24/8 28/8 NY 16/9 14/10 Syd 19/10 23/10 Liv 8/11 Stanlow 9-10/11

| SHIPS NAME | NET TONNAGE | PORT OF REGISTRY | CAPTAIN |
|---|---|---|---|
| | | | J. M. JACKSON |
| | 5772 | BELFAST | C. LAWSON 28/11/1940 |
| | | | E.J. INSTONE 4/12/1940 |
| | | | C. LAWSON 23/6/1941 |
| IROQUOIS (BRIT.) | | | E.J. INSTONE 11/11/1941 |

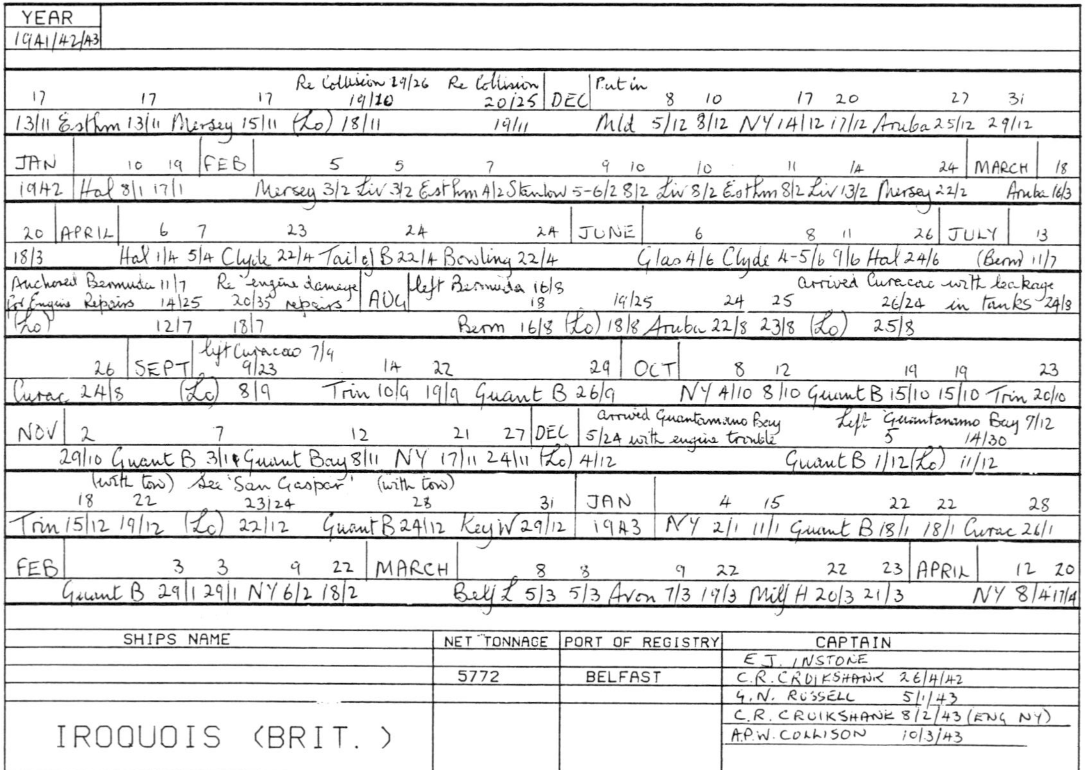
YEAR
1941/42/43

17 17 17 Re Collision 19/26 19/10 Re Collision 20/25 DEC Put in 8 10 17 20 27 31
13/11 Esthm 13/11 Mersey 15/11 (Lo) 18/11 19/11 Mld 5/12 8/12 NY 14/12 17/12 Aruba 25/12 29/12

JAN 10 19 FEB 5 5 7 9 10 10 11 14 24 MARCH 18
1942 Hal 8/1 17/1 Mersey 3/2 Liv 3/2 Esthm 4/2 Stenlow 5-6/2 8/2 Liv 8/2 Esthm 8/2 Liv 13/2 Mersey 22/2 Aruba 16/3

20 APRIL 6 7 23 24 24 JUNE 6 8 11 26 JULY 13
18/3 Hal 1/4 5/4 Clyde 22/4 Tail of B 22/4 Bowling 22/4 Glas 4/6 Clyde 4-5/6 9/6 Hal 24/6 (Berm) 11/7

Anchored Bermuda 11/7 for Engine Repairs 14/25 Re engine damage repairs 20/35 AUG Left Bermuda 16/8 18 19/25 24 25 arrived Curacao with leakage in tanks 26/24 24/8
(Lo) 12/7 18/7 Berm 16/8 (Lo) 18/8 Aruba 22/8 23/8 (Lo) 25/8

26 SEPT left Curacao 7/9 9/23 14 22 29 OCT 8 12 19 19 23
Curac 24/8 (Lo) 8/9 Trin 10/9 19/9 Guant B 26/9 NY 4/10 8/10 Guant B 15/10 15/10 Trin 20/10

NOV 2 7 12 21 27 DEC arrived Guantanamo Bay 5/24 with engine trouble Left Guantanamo Bay 7/12 5 14/30
29/10 Guant B 3/11 Guant Bay 8/11 NY 17/11 24/11 (Lo) 4/12 Guant B 1/12 (Lo) 11/12

(with tow) See 'San Gaspar' (with tow) 18 22 23/24 28 31 JAN 4 15 22 22 28
Trin 15/12 19/12 (Lo) 22/12 Guant B 24/12 Key W 29/12 1943 NY 2/1 11/1 Guant B 18/1 18/1 Curac 26/1

FEB 3 3 9 22 MARCH 8 8 9 22 22 23 APRIL 12 20
Guant B 29/1 29/1 NY 6/2 18/2 Belf L 5/3 5/3 Avon 7/3 19/3 Milf H 20/3 21/3 NY 8/4 17/4

| SHIPS NAME | NET TONNAGE | PORT OF REGISTRY | CAPTAIN |
|---|---|---|---|
| IROQUOIS (BRIT.) | 5772 | BELFAST | E.J. INSTONE<br>C.R. CRUIKSHANK 26/4/42<br>G.N. RUSSELL 5/1/43<br>C.R. CRUIKSHANK 8/2/43 (ENG NY)<br>A.P.W. COLLISON 10/3/43 |

YEAR
1943 | 44

28 28 | MAY | 1 4 8 8 15 | JULY | 12 Put in Norfolk 3/7 with plate cracked
Guant B 24/4 Guant B 24/4 Curac 27/4 1/5 Guant B 4/5 4/5 NY 11/5 8/7

(L) 12/36 left Norfolk 15/7 19/34 30 | AUG | 2 4 4 7 7 10+11
(Lo) 11/7 18/7 Clyde Anch 29/7 30/7 Tail o' B 2/8 Clyde Anch 2/8 5/8 Clyde Anch 5/8 8/8

25 | SEPT | 6 11 OHMS 13 28 | OCT | 19 29
NY 21/8 2/9 Hamp Rds 3/9 12/9/43 Hamp Rds 6/9 Alg 25/9 5/10 Bzta 7/10 25/10

29 | NOV | 26+6 | DEC | off OHMS 20 | JAN | 5 6 Re weather damage arrived 10/35 Hampton Rds 5/1
Mlt 26/10 22/11 15/12/43 NY 17/12 | 1944 | NY 1/1 NY 3/1 (Lo) 9/1

Left Hampton Rds 14/1 18/25 | FEB | 3 8 8 21 | MARCH | 11 14 17 18 28
17/1 Oran 1/2 4/2 Gib 5/2 16/2 NY 8/3 11/3 Hamp Rds 12/3 14/3 Fayal 25/3

APRIL | 3 17 | MAY | Re weather damage in 6/26 March 13 16 17 30 | JUNE | 5
31/3 NY 14/4 NY 4/5 NY 10/5 Hamp Rds 13/5 Hamp Rds 11/5 Gib 28/5 31/5

8 24 26 29 JULY | 6 6 12 13 13 15
Casa 5/6 A. U.S. Atlantic P 19/6 NY 19/6 25/6 Guant B 2/7 2/7 Carib 8/7 10/7 Trin 10/7 12/7

17 21 25 26 AUG | 24 | SEPT | 1 with tow 25 | OCT | 6
Aruba 14/7 19/7 Crist 21/7 Balb 23/7 Pearl Hbr 19/8 Fran 28/8 21/9 Pearl Hbr 12/10

| SHIPS NAME | NET TONNAGE | PORT OF REGISTRY | CAPTAIN |
|---|---|---|---|
| | | | APW COLLISON |
| | 5772 | BELFAST | JH PALMER-FELGATE 24/6/44 |
| IROQUOIS (BRIT.) | | | |

YEAR
1944/45

12 28 | NOV | 4 13 | DEC | 4 5 11
Pearl Hbr 6/10 Eniwetok 22/10 29/10 Ulithi 7/11 Kossol Rds 25/11 Ulithi 27/11 Eniwetok 6/12

22 | JAN | 11 31 | FEB | 1 9 (with tow) 23 26 | MARCH | 13 | MAY | 15
Pearl Hbr 19/12 | 1945 | Los A 28/11 27/1 Fran 29/1 4/2 Pearl Hbr 19/2 22/2 Los A 10/3 12/5

19 29 30 | JUNE | 2 13 16 | JULY | 3 4 9 9 24
Fran 15/5 25/5 Los A 26/5 31/5 Pearl Hbr 9/6 11/6 Balb 30/6 Crist 2/7 Curac 5/7 7/7 Pwle 23/7

25 25 25 | AUG | 25 27 28 28 30 30
Downs 24/7 Snd 24/7 Lo 24/7 Lo(c) 24/8 Snd 26/8 Lo 26/8 Humber 27/8 Hull 27/8 Hull 29/8

30 31 | SEPT | (ThamesH) 1 (ThamesH) 1 3 4 15 17 17 21
Spurn 29/8 Snd(p) 30/8 Lo(c) 31/8 Lo 30/8 Snd 1/9 Tyne 3/9 13/9 Dss 14/9 IW(p) 15/9 Gib(p) 19/9

OCT | 1 2 4 8 9 11 Re Windlass Repairs 12 15 17
Haifa 27/9 Haifa 30/9 P. Said 1/10 Haifa 4/10 6/10 Alx 7/10 (Haifa) 1/10 Alx 11/10 Haifa 12/10

18 20 22 | NOV | 14 16 20 20 21 24 26 26
Alx 4/10 17/10 Haifa 18/10 12/11 P. Said 13/11 Haifa 16/11 17/11 P. Said 18/11 20/11 Haifa 22/11 23/11

27 29 | DEC | (Lebanon) 1 1 3 6 10 10 11
P. Said 24/11 27/11 Trip 28/11 29/11 P. Said 1/12 P. Said 3/12 Haifa 6/12 7/12 Alx 8/12

| SHIPS NAME | NET TONNAGE | PORT OF REGISTRY | CAPTAIN | |
|---|---|---|---|---|
| | | | J. H. PALMER-FELGATE | |
| | 5772 | BELFAST | J. K. MACARTHUR | 16/4/45 |
| | | | A.P.W. COLLISTER | 25/7/45 |
| IROQUOIS (BRIT.) | | | J. H. DREW | 7/9/45 |

YEAR
1945/46

Re survey of Boiler
15 leakages of furnaces 24 27 28 31 | JAN | 3 8 10
(Haifa) 21/11 Alx 21/12 Haifa 23/12 26/12 Alx 29/12 | 1946 | Alx 1/1 Alx 6/1 9/1

15 16 22 26 | FEB | 1 7 7 11 13 20
P. Said 13/1 15/1 Alx 19/1 22/1 Haifa 26/1 Pir 3/2 Pir 30/1 P. Said 9/2 12/2 Alex 19/2

MARCH | 6 9 12 27 28 30 | APRIL | 17 20 | MAY | 2
3/3 Alx 7/3 Haifa 6/3 Alx 25/3 P. Said 26/3 Suez 27/3 Abad 14/4 17/4 Suez 30/4

Arrived Suez 30/4 with Windlass damage
2 approx delay 10 days 18 Repairs completed and 18 20 27
P. Said 1/5 17/5 vessel proceeded from Suez 17/5 Suez 17/5 P. Said 18/5 Gib 25/5

JUNE | 3 3 5 | JAN | 24 | FEB | 12
Ply 30/5 Liz 1/6 Glas 4/6 | 1947 | Glas 22/1 Troon 23/1

To be broken up Deleted from L.S.I. 14/2/47

| SHIPS NAME | NET TONNAGE | PORT OF REGISTRY | CAPTAIN |
|---|---|---|---|
| | | | J. H. DREW off 9/1/47 |
| | 5772 | BELFAST | |
| IROQUOIS (BRIT.) | | | |

# THE FAMILY TREE

GRANDFATHER William Mark Taphouse, an iron-plate worker and pump maker, met Mary Ann Smith, daughter of a funeral director, sometime in the 1860s. They were married on 17 April 1879 at the parish church of St Annes, Limehouse. The following year Mary gave birth to William Charles, on 12 February 1871, at 3 Victoria Place, St James Street, Limehouse. Alice Charlotte Sophia followed on 23 February 1873, at 26 Wonder Street, Limehouse; Henry Mark on 6 September 1875; and James Edward on 9 August 1877: both boys died within a few weeks of being born. Alfred John came into the world on 18 November 1880. Frederic George was born on 7 March 1882 at 143 Eastfield Street, Limehouse. The family then moved to 92 Locksley Street, Limehouse, and Herbert Walter was born on 19 September 1883. Arthur Philip was born on 7 March 1887 and, like two brothers before him, died within a few days of being born. Ernest Leonard arrived at Locksley Street on 28 April 1889. Grandfather William died in late 1894, when Ernest was only six.

His death plunged the family into poverty. I remember Herbert telling me that he could recall times when Ernest was sent to bed so that Mary could repair his only pair of trousers. By this time son William had finished his apprenticeship and Alice had been trained as a teacher. William decided that money was to be made by going to sea as a marine engineer, and that oil tanker companies paid the best wages. His mother never dispelled this idea, and William embarked on his career.

With Alice now teaching and William at sea, both putting their earnings into keeping their mother and brothers, the family managed to hold their heads above water financially. Mary, being an intelligent woman, made sure that each of the remaining boys (Alfred, Herbert, Fred and Ernest) should not be denied an education that might eventually lead to a good income. It was during Ernest's time at Thomas Street School that a lasting friendship with Fred Buckman and Bert Ellis began. Fred Buckman lived at 38 Locksley Street.

All the brothers in turn followed William to sea as engineers, and Mary told each of them that they were not to enjoy their time at sea or to mess about with women because they had to continue their studies while at sea and in port. She told them that financial security was gained only by those who held qualifications in their field. Each of the brothers sat for the Second Class Certificate of Competency (now known as the Board of Trade Certificate) and passed at the first attempt. Mary's advice was obviously heeded. This they could only sit when they had spent a total of at least fifteen months watch-keeping on foreign trade vessels. A further fifteen months watch-keeping had to elapse before they were able to sit for the First Class Certificate, (usually known as the Chief's ticket). Two of the brothers went on to take the Extra First Class Certificate.

The family was not without its tragedies. William died of kidney failure while home on leave in 1924. Fred too had his problems, while serving as Chief Engineer on the SS *Chesapeake.* In November 1911 the *Chesapeake* loaded at New York and set off for Algiers and Venice on 1 December. The *Chesapeake* for about five days endured stormy weather and rolled badly. At about 10.00 on 6 December there was an explosion in the vicinity of number two hatch on the port side. Flames at once shot up, followed by cases flying up into the sky. The ship's engine was put to half ahead and the wind was kept aft. Number two hatch cover had blown off as well as the tank lid to number four hatch, and the pump room was also on fire. By this time the Chinese crew aft were attempting to lower the lifeboats. The Master, armed with a revolver, ordered them out of the boats; some obeyed, but the rest remained in the starboard boat which was already in the water, and they had taken the 2nd Officer with them. It was with the utmost difficulty that the Chinese engine-room hands and stokers could be prevailed upon to go below so as to keep up the necessary head of steam. Although the steam extinguishing apparatus had been connected it could not be brought to bear. The fire by this time had made continual rapid progress. A fire that originated shortly after the explosion was found by Fred and the 1st Officer who both suffered terrible burns as a result. At 17.00 the Master gave the order to lower the remaining two lifeboats. By this time the bridge was on fire. The remaining officers and crew took to the boats and the Master lowered himself over the stern into one of them. One of the boats had its rudder smashed and was taken in tow by the other. The *Chesapeake* was now totally abandoned, and darkness setting in, the lifeboats stood by her all night. The position was lat.36°N long.48°W. At dawn the next morning they set sail and steered for the track of ships. For seven days they were at the mercy of the storms and waves. The provisions lasted well, but there was very little water, and several of the company including Fred were becoming delirious. Thirty-two Chinamen and the 2nd Officer who were in the other two boats were never found.

The first boat carried a red blanket at the mast as a distress signal. After seven days, during which they had traversed 300 miles, they sighted the smoke of a steamer, and they celebrated by drinking the remainder of their water supply. On 13 December they were picked up by the German steamer, the SS *Adamsturn* (of 5,000 tons, built in 1909 at Geestemunde and registered at Bremen). Some of the castaways were so weak that they had to be winched aboard in a boatswain's chair. It was by the merest chance that the boats had been seen, as they were three or four miles off the steamer's course. The 3rd Engineer of the *Adamsturn* had his attention drawn to something red in a blaze of sunshine, and investigation showed this to be the red seaman's blanket at the mast.

Fred and the 1st Officer shared a cabin on the *Adamsturn*. Fred lay there helpless and watched the 1st Officer die on the 15th. He was buried at sea on the 16th, and on the 23rd the *Adamsturn* landed the twenty-one survivors at Gibraltar where Fred was put into hospital. The cargo of the *Chesapeake* had consisted of petroleum in bulk, deodorized naphtha and turpentine in cases. Because of the weather encountered in the North Atlantic the cowl ventilators for the 'tween decks had been removed, the coamings plugged to prevent the shipping of sea water. The Board of Trade enquiry that followed in March 1912 concluded that there had been insufficient ventilation to the 'tween decks. It also concluded that there was a possibility that some of the cases of naphtha had got adrift during the heavy rolling of the ship, and by striking one another had caused sparks, which in turn had ignited the explosive vapour.

Article from *The Times*:

> The Board of Trade awarded a piece of plate to Mr. Adolf Hasenheier, Master of the *Adamsturn* of Bremen in recognition of his services to a portion of the shipwrecked crew of the SS *Chesapeake* of London, whom he rescued in the N. Atlantic on the 13/12/12 after their vessel had been burnt.

Fred spent most of his life working for Anglo-American Oil Co and was Chief Engineer of the SS *Saranac* when she was delivered new in 1917. He stayed with her until 1940, when Anglo-Am took him ashore as superintendent looking after ships that were being built at Haverton Hill on Tees shipyards. He retired due to ill health in 1942, after having had pneumonia twice. He died in 1964.

It took till the year 1994 for a further story to emerge about Fred as Chief Engineer of the *Saranac*. The ship suffered a major breakdown in the engine-room when the main circulating pump packed up when its engine

*The* Chesapeake.

*The* Adamstown.

was smashed beyond repair in mid-Atlantic. In those days there was no back-up pump and unfortunately, by design, no other pump could be brought into service. With no main circulating pump running, the main condenser could not be used, and the main engine could not be run. Fred contrived to run a cargo pump, pumping water from the fore-peak tank in the bow of the ship, up to deck level, along the length of deck, and manage to install pipes from deck down to the engine-room and on to the main condenser. In the engine-room there were pumps that were able to pump sea water into the fore-peak tank. This work took about two days. The quantity of water that was pumped through the main condenser was nowhere near as much as would have been delivered by the main circulating pump, but it was sufficient to enable a vacuum to be raised and the main engine started. The *Saranac* limped home at a speed of five knots.

Alice later on progressed to become headmistress of a Jewish girls' school in Christian Street, Aldgate. She must have made quite an impression at her interview because it was rather unusual for a gentile to hold such an appointment. She remained in this post till she retired, and died in 1949.

Ernest left school and Mary managed to find him a job as an apprentice engineer in a company known as Richmonds of Limehouse, where he started work at 2/6*d.* (twelve and a half pence) a week. Richmonds paid good wages to their workmen and this may have contributed to the company going bankrupt. Legislation in those days ensured that apprentices of a bankrupt company had, by law, to be taken on by other companies operating the same trades. Ernest was lucky enough to be taken on by Green and Silley Weirs, Blackwall Yard, who were a company that carried out shipbuilding and marine repairs. On arriving for work at the new company he was told that the wages for a third year apprentice were 1/6*d.* (seven and a half pence) a week less than he had been earning at Richmonds. The foreman told him that if Ernest proved to him that he was a capable apprentice he would pay the same rates that he received at Richmonds. They never did decrease his wages. At the end of his apprenticeship he stayed on at Greens as a journeyman while he applied to the shipping companies that operated tankers. He eventually joined Anglo-American Oil Company as a Junior Marine Engineer and joined the SS *Tamarac* at Purfleet on 15 April 1910.

Charles Arthur Green, jobbing builder and contractor of Ipswich, married Florence Maud Parker at St. Johns Church, Ipswich, on 30 May 1891, and they made their first home in Felixstowe as Charles was working in that area. Sydney Charles was born on 2 July 1892, at Upper Cavendish Road, Felixstowe. For a short time they lived in Thomlin Road, Ipswich,

P.S.M. SONS & CO

ANGLO AMERICAN OIL
CO LTD

TELEGRAPHIC ADDRESS
"MAINTOP, LONDON."

Steam Ship "Tamarac"
Port San Francisco
Date July 12th. 1913.

This is to Certify that Mr E. L. Taphouse has served as Fourth Engineer on above named vessel from July 13th. 1910 to May 16th. 1913 and as Third Engineer from May 17th. 1913 until present date, when I leave him still serving in same capacity.

During the above named period I have at all times found him Strictly Sober, attentive to his duties and a Conscientious Workman, and can recommend him to any one as such.

Yours Respectfully
A. A. Jarbes
Chief Engineer.

P.S. Vessels name is now changed to "Sequoya".

Y. J. Archbold
Acting Master

and finally settled in a house in Hatfield Road, Ipswich. Myrtie Maud was born on 19 November 1893, Audley Arthur on 30 August 1894, Raymond Ralph on 30 June 1895, Ivy May on 1 September 1903 and Eric on 18 December 1911. By this time Charles Green was a well-known builder and contractor and a member of Ipswich Town Council.

Bert Ellis, Ernest Taphouse's schoolfriend from Limehouse, married Myrtie on 13 October 1920 and for some time lived in Rotterdam because of his job with General Steam Navigation Co. They were married in Ipswich, which was where the Green family lived. One of the times in 1923 that Ernest was in Rotterdam (with the *Iroquois*) he met up with Bert and Myrtie, and also Myrtie's sister Ivy, who was staying with them on holiday. This was the first meeting of Ivy and Ernest. One time in 1925 when Ernest docked at Purfleet, he met up with Bert, who was by this time living in Ilford, and went back with him to his house. Ivy just happened to be there. They got on well; this must have been quite an achievement, for Ernest was a shy man. Writing letters had never been a difficulty for Ernest.

92 Locksley Street,<br>Limehouse,<br>London. E14.<br>Oct.8th 1927

Dear Ivy,

I hope I may still address you thus! Guess who is writing to you. No! don't turn to the back of the letter; be a sport and wade through it.

It is a long time since we met but I often get news of you from Myrtie and Bert, and early last week your sister informed me that you had mentioned me in one of your letters to her. Such a pleasant surprise prompts me to write this little note.

During the last few weeks I have made several journeys to Beehive Lane and have had the pleasure of meeting your Mother. Little Joyce is quite well again now and speaks of her railway accident as quite a trivial affair. What a narrow escape she had, and what a shock it must have been to Myrtie—after all her other troubles. Really! I think Myrtie is one girl in a million to have borne all her trials with such fortitude. I trust that they have seen the last of their troubles and that good times are in store for them.

Bert is much the same as ever—still full of life, still keen on music, and I should imagine, still a little fiery when provoked. Do you remember that little squabble, in which we all took part, at the flat in

Rotterdam? I believe it was the night before you left for home. However they are a loyal and happy little family and we are always very pleased to see them; in fact, a deep affection seems to have taken root between Myrtie and my sister. I much regret, that owing to the very short spells which I get in London when the ship arrives home, I am unable to see them as I would wish.

We are usually away seven weeks and seldom get more than three nights in London. Naturally, I am getting very tired of this and contemplate transferring my affections to another company, whose ships do not go away for such long periods.

I am just concluding a seven weeks holiday; four of which I spent in France with my sister. We were in Paris for a few days and then went south to Provence. Had glorious weather—nothing but brilliant sunshine the whole of the time. Provence is full of interesting old cities, most of which were built by the Romans. We had a most enjoyable time and I had but one thing to regret, viz—that we had not been able to spend the whole summer there. Some people are greedy! Myrtie and Bert are looking forward to a trip there some day.

Now! I hope I have not bored you with this somewhat lengthy epistle. If it is not asking too much would you drop me a line? I should be so pleased to hear from you.

Myrtie tells me you will shortly be spending a week-end with her. I wonder if I shall see you. This ship is in London now and will be proceeding to the Tyne for dry-docking. There may be an opportunity for me to get down home for one week-end. This, however, is very uncertain as I am unable at present to say how long the ship will be in dock.

s/s *Iroquois*
Later.

Have just rejoined the ship. I spent an hour or two at Beehive Lane this evening—all are well. They were asking me if I could get home this next week-end. I hardly think that this can be managed as we shall not arrive at the Tyne until Friday morning, but if the ship is still in dock I hope to get down on the following week-end. viz 15th and 16th.

Will close now as I am sure this awful scrawl must be straining your eyes.

With kind regards and best wishes

Yours sincerely
Ernie

If you write—and I do hope you will—please address your letter to
E.L. Taphouse
Chief Engineer s/s *Iroquois*
c/o Smiths Dry Dock
North Shields.

Ernest asked Ivy to write to him while he was at sea. They frequently corresponded by letter. A few trips later Ernest docked at Purfleet, and asked Bert to arrange a trip down to Ipswich. This was duly arranged, and they met yet again. Ernest then travelled alone down to Ipswich to met Ivy on each occasion that he was able. On one of these occasions Ivy was not at home when Ernest arrived at Hatfield Road. He was let in by Myrtie who sat with him for about half an hour before Ivy arrived home. 'Don't you ever leave me alone with that man again,' said Myrtie to Ivy. 'I couldn't get a word out of him.' From that meeting onwards, Ernest often journeyed down to Ipswich to meet Ivy and on a few occasions in 1928 and '29 Ivy and her parents travelled down to Purfleet to see Ernest on board the *Iroquois*. Ernest, to most people, appeared a very quiet and undemonstrative man. Because of continual report-writing, which was part of his job as Chief Engineer, he had no difficulty in writing plenty of letters to Ivy. He wrote the following letter to her three hours before they married.

Elsworth
Britannia Road,
Ipswich.
8.55 am Sat. Sept.7th 1929

My Own Little Darling Girl,

Our happy hour approaches . . . and I feel sure, a happy life is to follow. Our two years of courtship have been very happy years, haven't they darling? During the last few minutes I have been running through the happy times we have had together. They will always be happy memories; as will our last little 'engaged' talk of last night.

Darling, throughout these two years you have shown me a kind nature and loving disposition. These are the essentials darling, and I face the future without fear of any sort. A 'thousand and one' little things . . . show me that I have found a girl who is a real treasure. I cannot help repeating something I have told you so many times. 'Your love, my darling, is the best and sweetest thing that ever happened in my life.'

Did you sleep well last night, dear? I had a very good night. Ethel is looking after me! Darling you are giving me 'in-laws' who are simply splendid.

Have you heard about last nights 'do'? And now, darling, Ray will soon be returning, to take me to the barbers, so I will close this short note . . . my last as your fiance!

Oh, my love! I am waiting for the next few hours to pass, to see your dear little face beneath your veil, when you reach my side.

Darling, I love you: shall always love you, and pray that I be a worthy husband to you. We shall be sweethearts all our lives. xxx

With all my love, thoughts and kisses
Yours for ever
Ernie

They married on 7 September 1929 at Wesleyan Chapel, Alan Road, Ipswich, after a two-year courtship. They spent their honeymoon in the south of France.

The following was an article in the *Ipswich Times* the following week:

TAPHOUSE – GREEN

The wedding took place on Saturday, at Alan Road Wesleyan Church, of Ernest Leonard Taphouse, youngest son of Mrs. Taphouse, of 92, Locksley Street, Limehouse, London, to Miss Ivy May Green, youngest daughter of Mr. and Mrs. Charles A. Green of "Woodcote" 56, Hatfield Road, Ipswich. The bride's father is a member of Ipswich Town Council, and a well-known builder in Ipswich. The bridegroom is Chief Engineer of the T.S.S. *Iroquois*, one of the largest vessels of the Anglo-American Oil Company's fleet. There was a large attendance of the relatives and friends of the two families.

The bride was charmingly attired in chenille georgette, trimmed with a girdle and embroidered with a lover's knot of diamante. Her tulle-embroidered veil was fastened with a coronet of orange blossoms, and she carried a sheaf of Madonna lilies. She was attended by four bridesmaids, and her little nephew, Master Dennis Green, in a purple velvet suit, acted a page.

The adults were Miss Pearla Paskall, a cousin of the bride, and Miss Vera Broughton, whose frocks were of mauve crepe de chine, and each wore a silver chain with amethyst pendant, the gift of the bridegroom, and the young girl nieces of the bride, Joyce Ellis and Jean Green,

were dressed in pale pink crepe de chine. They wore a silver chain with amethyst drop.

The page wore a gold tie-pin, which was a gift from the bridegroom. All the four ladies wore silver lace Dutch caps, and carried shower bouquets of Northcliffe carnations and Victoria pansies. Mr F.W. Buckman, of London, acted as best man.

The ceremony was performed by the Rev. P.M. Despres, the minister of the church, assisted by the Rev. C.O. George, vicar of St. Augustine's Church, Felixstowe Road, Ipswich, and the bride was given away by her father. Mr. James A. Ellis, organist, of Holy Trinity Church, Ilford, presided at the organ, and played appropriate music before and after the ceremony.

After the service, a reception was held in the school hall, adjoining the church from which the bride and bridegroom received a hearty send-off on their journey to the South of France. The bride travelled in a grey silk coat, trimmed with fox fur, and wore a blue hat.

Ivy and Ernest received a 120-piece canteen of cutlery as a wedding present from the *Iroquois*. On the lid was an inlaid brass plate which said: To Ernie and Ivy Taphouse on the occasion of their wedding 7th of September 1929, from his brother officers of T.S.S. *Iroquois*.

They decided to settle for a house that was within easy travelling distance of Purfleet. One in Deynecourt Gardens, Upminster, proved suitable and they settled in there within a few months of being married, and named it *Vaucluse* after the favourite place they had been to on honeymoon.

Anne Margaret was born to them on 6 August 1932, and on several occasions baby Anne was able to go on board the *Iroquois* for a few days. By this time Ernest felt that the time was drawing near that he should put the life at sea behind him and settle down in a job ashore. As a half-way point he did stand-by duty on several ships that were laid up in the King

Harry's Passage of the River Fal, Cornwall. This was initially on the *Iroquois*, and was followed by the 6,921-ton *Invergordon* built in 1923 and belonging to the British Mexican Oil Company, (a further subsidiary of the Anglo-American Oil Co.) During this time baby Anne fell out of the cot on board ship and broke her arm; it was two days before this was noticed. He finally quit life at sea amidst a time of high unemployment, when Masters sailed as AB seamen and Chief Engineers sailed as Junior Engineers, and settled down in a job as maintenance engineer at Sherwood Paints at Barking. This job was an ungracious one after the life that he had been accustomed to, but he stayed in that job until he retired in December 1955. Ivy suffered two miscarriages before son Leonard Charles was born on 2 September 1939. War broke out the next day (now you know why it started), but that did not stop Gwendoline Mary being born on 13 June 1941.

Grandmother Mary Ann Taphouse died in March 1931, Ernest died in August 1968 and Ivy in August 1992.

# HIS CAREER AT SEA

THE long three-year trip that Ernest did was followed by one trip in the 3,368-ton *Wapello* sailing out of Birkenhead to New York and back to Belfast. After a couple of months leave, he had his first spell of working with the 'Twins' and was posted to the *Navahoe* on 3 October 1914, as 1st Engineer in charge of Auxiliary Engines. The *Navahoe* did not have any main engines for propelling purposes but had generators, winches and many cargo pumps.

Ernest stayed on the *Navahoe* till 23 March 1915. After two months leave he joined the *Iroquois* as Second Engineer on 6 May, and fell in love with the ship from that day on. She was the hottest ship that he sailed on but he felt that the *Iroquois* was HIS. His one ambition was to make it fully his, and this could only be achieved by becoming Chief Engineer of the *Iroquois*. In total he did sixteen transatlantic trips on her and his love of the *Iroquois* in some way probably prevented him being promoted. He eventually left the *Iroquois* on 31 October 1918, at the end of his three-year articles, signing off at Port Arthur and sailing home on a steamer for a two months' leave, after which he joined the 2,075-ton tanker *Suwanee* as Chief Engineer, at a wage of nearly thirty pounds a month.

The first trip on the *Suwanee* was OHMS and lasted for ten weeks. This consisted of crossing the Atlantic and refuelling some of the British fleet that was stationed out there at that time. He stayed on the *Suwanee* for a further two trips, one to the Baltic to Partille, Gothenburg, and one to the US Gulf. After a two month leave he joined the 1,833-ton *Genesee* as relieving Chief Engineer for a three-month trip to Tampico on the Mexican Gulf. (This ship had been attacked several times during the war by U-boats. Two attacks were made on the North Sea on 23 March 1917 and six months later on 27 September. In both attacks the torpedoes missed. Then on 1 January 1918, and again in the North Sea, the *Genesee* was hit. She listed heavily to port, and the Master sent most of his crew to an escorting patrol boat.

The *Genesee* eventually righted herself and with four remaining crew was brought to Hartlepool. She suffered further damage, again in the North Sea, on 21 July 1918, but still managed to reach port. The *Genesee* was later

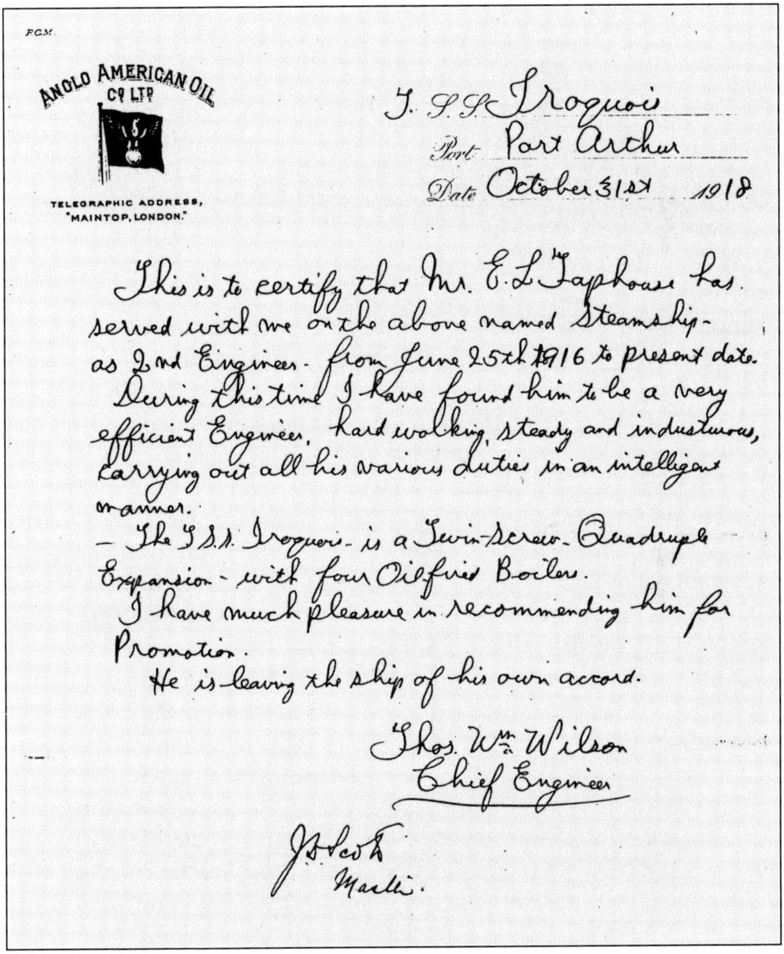

P.G.M.

ANGLO AMERICAN OIL
CO LTD

TELEGRAPHIC ADDRESS,
"MAINTOP, LONDON."

T. S.S. Iroquois
Port Port Arthur
Date October 31st 1918

This is to certify that Mr. E. L. Taphouse has served with me on the above named Steamship- as 2nd Engineer- from June 25th 1916 to present date.
During this time I have found him to be a very efficient Engineer, hard working, steady and industrious, carrying out all his various duties in an intelligent manner.
- The T.S.S. Iroquois- is a Twin-Screw- Quadruple- Expansion- with four Oil fired Boilers.
I have much pleasure in recommending him for Promotion.
He is leaving the ship of his own accord.

Thos. Wm. Wilson
Chief Engineer

J.S. Scott
Master.

Suwanee. *(Courtesy of Esso.)*

*SS* Delaware.

transferred to Hamble Spit, Southampton, where she was used as a bunkering hulk, and stayed there till 1924 when she was scrapped.)

The bigger ships beckoned, and he joined the 4,473-ton *Tuscarora*, a power tanker for her tonnage, on 26 July 1919 as 2nd Engineer. Three transatlantic trips later he joined the 2,469-ton *Delaware* as Chief Engineer on 28 February 1921. Ten years previously brother William had been Chief Engineer of the *Delaware*. The *Delaware* traded between Tilbury and the US Gulf ports and back to the northern UK ports, (Birkenhead and Avonmouth) but he still had his sights set on the *Iroquois*. The chance of the position of Chief Engineer of the *Iroquois* came on 5 May 1922, when he joined her at Rotterdam as the regular Chief Engineer. The *Iroquois* became HIS ship. As Chief Engineer of a ship it was his choice to stay with that ship. If he decided to miss a trip in order to take leave, a relief Chief Engineer would be put on board, but Ernest had the right to rejoin the *Iroquois* at the end of his leave. He stayed with the *Iroquois* for fifty-two transatlantic crossings, which finished on 18 December 1934. His total voyages with the 'Twins' numbered seventy-one.

He stayed on the *Iroquois* when she was laid up in the River Fal.

# THE STORIES OF HIS SHIPS

My father's first year's service as a marine engineer started when he joined the 3,318-ton *Tamarac*, on 15 April 1910. His first voyage opened up a new world to him as he sailed across to New York and back. The next trip started at North Shields on the Tyne, across to New York, through the Mediterranean Sea and through the Suez Canal. They passed the tiny island of Perim at the southernmost tip of the Red Sea on 12 September, and on to Singapore and Hong Kong and back to Rotterdam.

Anglo-American Oil Co at that time were able to transport more oil than could be consumed in the UK and they were turning their attention to the Far East, and from 1905 onwards they were increasing their fleet in the Pacific and the Indian Oceans. On 15 December 1910 he rejoined the same ship not knowing to where he was to travel.

On their way across to New York they were in wireless contact with the liner SS *Mauritania*. When the *Tamarac* reached New York they took on a cargo of kerosene and they were told that the ship had been taken over for a three-year charter by the Tank Storage and Carriage Company, a subsidiary company of Anglo-American Oil Co. They travelled on through the Suez Canal, down into the Indian Ocean, round to Calcutta and on to Singapore.

A three-year period was the longest time that anyone at that time could be kept away from home under Mercantile articles. Father told me that the middle year was by far the worst. The first year was just a long trip, the last year was for looking forward to getting home (only a few more months!) There were no talking points for the middle years. He was found to be such a good engineer that he was promoted from Junior to 4th Engineer after only one voyage, and from 4th Engineer to 3rd Engineer on 17 May 1913.

For the whole of the three years the *Tamarac* plied around the Pacific and Indian Ocean, between San Francisco and Hong Kong, Hong Kong and Calcutta, and back to Borneo, sometimes San Francisco to Shanghai, Hankow and Japan, or the Philippines and on to Hong Kong, a trans-Pacific trip of about sixteen to twenty days. They usually loaded at either San Francisco or Balik Papan in Borneo.

*First trip for Ernest on SS* Tamarac, *1910. Ernest in middle, front row.*

*Officers aboard SS* Tamarac *in 1911 in the Pacific. Ernest front row, left.*

Borneo at that time was a major oil-producing country, to the extent that an oil refinery was built at Balik Papan.

One of these trips took thirty-nine days, when they met the fiercest storm that he ever encountered at sea, between Singapore and San Francisco. From what he said, it sounded more like a typhoon. They left Singapore on 15 March and arrived at San Francisco on 24 May. He said that they just pointed the ship into the storm and kept going. They became worried because the bunkers were running low. They had coal-fired boilers; if they had been oil-fired boilers at least they could have fuelled the boilers with part of the cargo! However, they did make port.

The *Tamarac* was renamed *Sequoya* on 11 July 1913 and from then onwards became part of the fleet of Tank Storage and Carriage Co.

On or around 21 June 1913, somewhere out in Borneo, Father was walking alone along a road when he came across a large gorilla that was chained up outside a public house. Father, feeling perfectly safe as the gorilla was chained, went quite close to it. When he was very near, the gorilla's hand shot out and grabbed Father's wrist. Father said that it was a good solid grip, not blood-constricting, but one that he knew that he could not wrestle free from. From the size of the gorilla I do not think he would have tried anyway. The gorilla stared at Father for about twenty minutes solid while he held on to his wrist. Gradually Father felt the grip lessening, and the second that the gorilla let go, Father snatched his wrist away. Apparently not quite quickly enough, as the gorilla grabbed his wrist again. This time it was only a ten-minute staring and holding session. When the gorilla eventually let go, my father very slowly moved away.

On one occasion in Singapore, my father returned to his cabin on the *Tamarac* to find a very large spider stuck on the deck-head (landlubbers call it ceiling). The spider's body was about the size of the palm of his hand, rather large by any standards. He didn't want to touch it as he did not know if it would bite, or whether it was poisonous or not. He took off his plimsoll and whacked the spider with it. Splat! and all its guts were disembowelled on to my father's chest. By the way, my father always told this story at the meal table.

Ernest paid off in San Francisco on 20 December 1913 at the end of his three-year articles, and began the long trip home to the UK. He journeyed through the Nevada desert to Salt Lake City, over the Rockies to Cheyenne. On to Omaha via Nebraska, through Iowa and Illinois to Chicago. Bear in mind that this journey had been for eight days continuous. He took a break for about two days sightseeing before joining another train to New York, where he caught a passenger steamer to London. He arrived back at Locksley Street in the middle of January 1914.

Between 1910 and 1915 it was the custom of all the company's ships, when coasting around India, to make the south coast ports their first ports of call. Because the ships then discharged only a few hundred tons of oil at a time, often into barrels or into tanker barges, there was an enormous amount of handling to be carried out. To make this handling easier, several men were then taken on board to assist with this task. They were known as 'boys' and remained on the ship till it reached its last port of call on the Indian coast. Here they were paid off, and remained in port until they were able to join another ship travelling on the opposite route.

On one such occasion they were about to be paid off at an east Indian port, probably Calcutta. The ship's purser had a large trestle table on the quay piled high with bank notes and all his paperwork spread out with the line of 'boys' waiting. One of the crew ran down the ship's ladder to tell the purser that he was urgently required on board the ship. This put the purser in quite a quandary. As he was alone he could not pick up all the money and paperwork and go back to the ship, nor could he leave it on the table unattended. His solution was to take out his glass eye, lay it on the table facing the line of 'boys' and then say to the eye: 'Eye, watch dem nigger.' The line of 'boys' fled. They had never seen a white man who could take his eye out!

After a somewhat wild party on board the *Tamarac*, one of the crewmen was well tanked up and decided that he could do a balancing act on the bulwark around the poop deck. He managed to get up on to the bulwark and started to walk along it with arms outstretched. He was not able to do this for very long as he overbalanced and instead of falling on the deck, fell overboard while the ship was in motion. The engines were stopped and a boat lowered. They were in shark-infested waters at the time, and although the area was thoroughly searched, he was never found.

Because of the way in which he had been inspired by his mother, Ernest sat for his Second Class Engineer's Certificate as soon as he had completed the qualifying time of fifteen months watch-keeping. A further fifteen months elapsed before he could sit for his First Class Certificate. He sat the exam on 6 January 1913, as soon as he had completed the qualifying time, and at the age of twenty-three years he was the youngest holder of a Chief's Ticket at that time. When he held his first post as Chief Engineer on the 2,075-ton *Suwanee*, he was only twenty-nine, and at that age and time was the youngest Chief Engineer at sea.

On another of the trips halfway across the Pacific, they had a hawk come down on the deck. Remember that they were a week away from land. The hawk landed on the deck and sat on its haunches, obviously exhausted. One of the crew took out a dish of water to the hawk, who immediately started drinking from it. The same crewman then brought out some meat from the galley and held it between his fingers in front of the hawk. The hawk pecked the man on the back of the hand so hard that it drew blood. The crewman dropped the meat, only then did the hawk eat it. This story adds a new dimension to the adage: 'Don't bite the hand that feeds you'.

One day my father was out walking in Borneo with one of his brother officers from the *Tamarac*. The road that they were on ran alongside a jungle. They found a wide track that left the road and ran into the jungle, and being naturally curious they turned down the track and continued on their walk. They kept walking till nearly dusk before they decided to turn back, by which time the track had petered out, and they were some way into the jungle. When they started walking back they realized that the track was not as visible as it was on the outward journey.

The pair of them then walked all night but were unable to get any bearings whatsoever till sunrise. A further two hours walking found them back on track to civilization, and a return to the ship. My father lost a gold pocket watch in the jungle but never went back to retrieve it. When they eventually found a village, the people told them that they had walked through an area that was infested with a local type of rattlesnake.

In his early days at sea on the *Iroquois*, the ship was in New York harbour for a few days. It just happened that Herbert's ship docked there at about the same time. They met up with each other and took a trip to Coney Island, which was set in one of the New York suburbs and was a very large amusement park and funfair. Ernest and Herbert went on the Big Wheel. In those days it was known as a Ferris Wheel. When the big wheel stopped to let riders off they were in the boat that was at the top of the wheel. The brakes stuck on and the wheel refused all attempts at turning it. The people that were in the lower boats were brought down by means of ladders that were brought to the scene, but Ernest and Herbert stayed up there all night till about 6.30 in the morning. By that time they had removed the part of the engine that drove the wheel and the wheel was pulled round by hand. They were given back their ride money and were treated to a hearty breakfast before they returned to their ships.

On 3 September 1920, while Father was serving as 2nd Engineer, the officers on the bridge of the *Tuscarora*, about 900 miles from the Azores,

*The* Tuscarora. *(Courtesy of Esso.)*

spotted a ship in distress. This turned out to be the *Elias Issaias* which was in danger of sinking. Some of the Greek crew had already abandoned ship and were in the lifeboats; these were taken aboard the *Tuscarora*. The Master, the engineer and three of his crew had stayed on the vessel and an attempt to tow the vessel was made in the afternoon.

Thirty minutes later the vessel started sinking and had to be abandoned, at a position lat.40° 41N long. 41° 52W. They brought on board the Master and twenty crew members that were in the lifeboats and attempted another tow. My father as 2nd Engineer was sent across to the vessel with other officers from the *Iroquois* to look to see if the vessel was worth towing. My father said that the boilers were salted up, but reckoned that they could still be got going with a supply of steam from the *Tuscarora*. They managed to tow her for a further 273 miles before the *Elias Issaias* finally foundered in bad weather. They brought the ship's company back to Purfleet. It later turned out that the *Elias Issaias* was a screw steamer of wooden construction of 1,495 tons, equipped with a small compound expansion engine, and was registered at Piraeus. She was captained by the owner, E. Issaias and was 225 feet long and 35 feet wide. She had been built the previous year and begun her voyage with a cargo of coal from Baltimore, and was bound for Piraeus.

When he joined the *Iroquois* on 5 June 1917 they were not told where the ship was going to, other than her first port of call was to be Colon. The whole of the ship's company took part in a sweepstake, which was based on the final destination and the expected date of arrival. They finally

*A couple of surviving examples of his copperwork. The plate measures 12 inches across and the match box, which has a sandpaper inset, is about 3½ inches high.*

docked at San Francisco and Ernest won the sweepstake outright. The trip went on till 4 October 1918. When he reached Locksley Street he told Mary that he had taken part in a bet on board the ship. 'Disgusting,' said Mary, 'all gambling is evil.' 'I did win,' said Ernest. 'It's alright then,' said his mother, 'if you win.'

My father always had a high opinion of American dentists. So after having had all his teeth removed, he decided to have his dentures made in New York. He visited a dentist in New York and had the impressions made, and deposit paid, telling the dentist that he would collect the dentures the next time he docked in New York (about a month later).

The *Iroquois* returned to the UK, discharged, and started on the return trip. Halfway across the Atlantic they were in radio contact with one of the company's other ships homeward bound. The message was addressed to my father, and it said, 'Found a set of teeth on the dentist's bench with my name on them, but they didn't fit.' One of his brothers had by chance visited the same dentist in New York.

The *Iroquois* was a unique ship in many ways. The small oil-baths and drip trays around the engine room were all made from either brass or copper sheet; she even had brass handrails. My father had a keen interest in beaten copper and brass-work. He spent much of his spare time in this pastime. On several occasions in port, the Engineering Superintendent from Anglo-American queried the amount of brass and copper sheet that was ordered by the *Iroquois*, as it appeared to be excessive when compared to the other ships in the company's fleet. My father's answer was that no one would want to spoil the looks of the engine room by putting in a drip tray made from mild steel when all the other ones were made from brass or copper.

By the time my father left the sea, after twenty-four years, he had built up a wonderful collection of beaten and planished brass and copper-ware. During his time at sea he had taught himself to carve in copper. His designs were somewhat limited, and usually consisted of a leaf or lily pattern. He also, using books as a guide, taught himself the art of enamelling. He did admit, though, that he never did master the knack of doing more than one colour at a time.

In 1928 Cousin Bertie decided on making a career as a marine engineer, and joined Anglo-American Oil Co after having served his apprenticeship. The company decided to place Bertie on the *Iroquois* on 14 April. As it happened he was placed with two other junior engineers who had both done at least one trip at sea already. Father pleaded with the company to remove Bertie from his chain of responsibility as he did not want to show

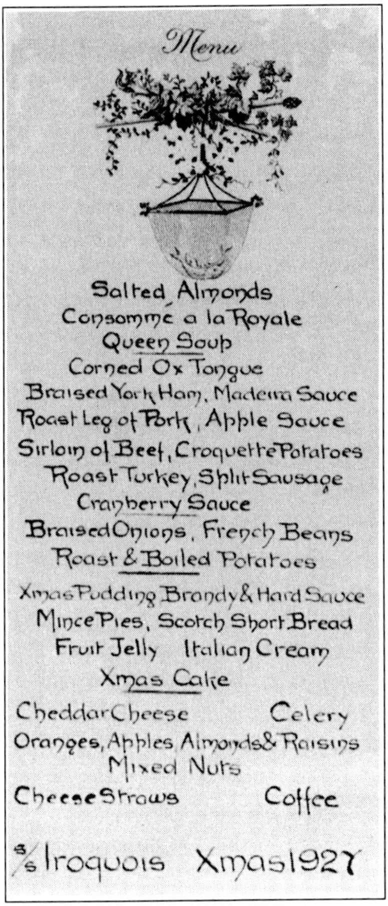
Menu
Salted Almonds
Consomme a la Royale
Queen Soup
Corned Ox Tongue
Braised York Ham, Madeira Sauce
Roast Leg of Pork, Apple Sauce
Sirloin of Beef, Croquette Potatoes
Roast Turkey, Split Sausage
Cranberry Sauce
Braised Onions, French Beans
Roast & Boiled Potatoes
Xmas Pudding Brandy & Hard Sauce
Mince Pies, Scotch Short Bread
Fruit Jelly Italian Cream
Xmas Cake
Cheddar Cheese Celery
Oranges, Apples, Almonds & Raisins
Mixed Nuts
Cheese Straws Coffee
S/S Iroquois Xmas 1927

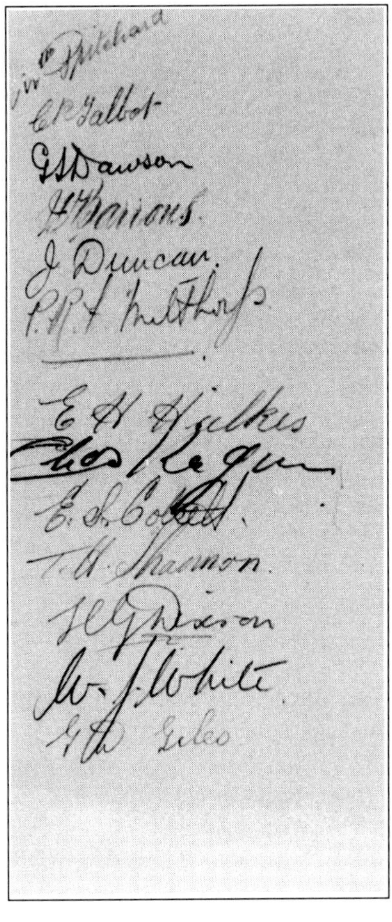

any favours to Bertie; these pleadings fell on deaf ears, and Bertie sailed with the *Iroquois* for five voyages to the US Gulf ports.

At the end of Bertie's fifth voyage, Father was asked which out of the three junior engineers he would recommend for promotion. This put him in an embarrassing position. I remember him telling me that Bertie was a far better engineer than the other two engineers put together. Father recommended Bertie, and Bertie was then promoted to 4th Engineer and left to join the *Tamarac*. Father wrote in to the company requesting that they never put him in the same embarrassing position again. Bertie stayed with the *Tamarac* till 6 March 1932, by which time he had been promoted to 3rd Engineer. By this time he had taken both his tickets. He then transferred to motor vessels and took his Motor Endorsements, the first in the family.

My father led his life as a Chief Engineer as a bit of a recluse, often spending many hours in the engine-room workshop, amusing himself with his copper-work. When he was not doing this he was, in conjunction with two other officers, often engrossed in writing a ship's magazine. This was known as 'Cam-Frags', no idea how the name originated, and they enjoyed the liberty of taking the mickey out of almost every member of the ship's company. He would carefully print each page on a special paper, and copies would be made using hectographic jelly, which I'm sure he used to manufacture himself. He also printed out the Christmas menus. The one that is shown on the page opposite is the one that he sent to my mother; note the G.S. Dawson, mentioned later in the *Cheyenne* saga. That Christmas day they were somewhere near the Gulf of Mexico. They had cleared Beachy Head on 7 December and arrived at Houston on 7 January.

Bertie once told me that he sometimes met Father at Locksley Street, sometimes they left there together and took the same train to Tilbury, but they sat in separate carriages on the journey to Tilbury in case any of the other crew members were on the same train. Apparently it was not the done thing for a Junior Engineer to be seen travelling with his Chief Engineer, especially if the Chief Engineer was his uncle. Bertie's son also told me that Bertie had told him that on his first trip Bertie was complaining to other Junior Engineers that he could not afford to buy himself a pair of boots for engine-room work. (He was one of those poorly paid Junior Engineers.) That evening when Bertie was sitting on deck in the darkness talking to other crew members, a pair of boots came sailing through the darkness and landed at Bertie's feet. Bertie guessed that they were from Father, but it was not the done thing to thank one's relations.

Cousin Bertie was on the afternoon 12 to 4 watch, and Father was silver-soldering a copper cigarette box over the forge. The forge had a hearth with coke in it and a set of foot-operated bellows underneath, and was situated in the engine-room workshop. The *Iroquois'* engine-room was a hot one at the best of times (Cousin Bertie reckoned that it was the hottest that he had ever worked in). Bertie could see that my father was working in the workshop, and said to himself: 'No way will he get me to help him in the workshop, the engine-room is hot enough without standing over a hot forge.'

At the end of the watch Bertie climbed the ladders to go up out of the engine-room; this meant passing the workshop where Father was working. Bertie ducked down below the level of the bulkhead, so that he could not be seen, however, he did have to pass an open doorway. As he did so a voice boomed out, 'Taphouse, I've got a little job I want you to help me with.' It was Bertie's job to operate the bellows.

Bertie always said that my father was a hard man to work for, a good engineer who would always listen to others and was, above all, always fair. Bertie also said that everyone's trust in Father was so great that many of the men on the ship gave their wages to him for safe-keeping. The skipper at that time gave Father the keys to his spirits locker to prevent him over-drinking.

One of the cadets who served on the *Iroquois* as a deck cadet for four years wrote this about my father: 'He was a fine figure of a man, walked in an upright manner, very much the gentleman. I saw him every day from August 1926 to August 1930, but I cannot remember seeing him engaged in an animated conversation with anyone. He was very quiet and kept himself to himself. He used to walk up and down the poop deck for his daily exercise, but always alone. He was well liked by his staff and by everyone on board. I used to think he was of a shy disposition. Each evening at sea he played cards in the Captain's cabin. No one ever joined in, nor for that matter was ever invited to join in.'

One Christmas time in port, (this was a rare occasion) one of the crew climbed the foremast of the *Navahoe* to put up a Christmas tree. No sooner had he tied it to the foremast than he fell to his death on the deck.

When the *Iroquois* was running solo, she was not really considered to be an economic proposition. To make her cargo-carrying capacity greater the fore-peak and the after-peak tanks were used as cargo tanks. This reduced the amount of fresh water that could be carried. Because of this the ship's company was always kept short of water. They therefore adopted a save water campaign. If they washed themselves in a basin and the water was not dirty, the plug was not pulled, so that the next person could use the water again. My father kept this annoying habit till the day he died.